AF478886

Welcome to Design Miami/2013

Welcome to Design Miami/2013, the global forum for design. December's fair presents masterworks from the twentieth century until today from the world's most influential design galleries alongside a progressive program of Satellite exhibitions, Design Talks and a new Design Commission from New York-based architectural practice formlessfinder.

At the core of the Design Miami/forum is the gallery program, which includes a strategic selection of galleries from around the globe chosen for their efforts to develop a comprehensive appreciation of movements, designers and individual works that have shaped design history.

Design Miami/2013 welcomes four new galleries to December's program: Antonella Villanova from Florence, Fine Art Silver from Brussels, Galleria Rossana Orlandi from Milan, Heritage Gallery from Moscow and Louisa Guinness Gallery from London.

In addition to these exhibitors, the fair's roster of prestigious international galleries includes: Carpenters Workshop Gallery, Casati Gallery, Cristina Grajales Gallery, Demisch Danant, gabrielle ammann// gallery, Galerie Downtown-François Laffanour, Galerie kreo, Galerie Maria Wettergren, Galerie Patrick Seguin, Galerie Jacques Lacoste, Gallery SEOMI, Hostler Burrows, Jason Jacques Gallery, Jousse Entreprise, Magen H Gallery, Mark McDonald, Moderne Gallery, Pierre Marie Giraud, Priveekollektie, R 20th Century and Sebastian + Barquet.

Complementing the main gallery shows, Design Miami's Design On/Site Galleries launch new work in installation-driven solo shows. Each On/Site expresses a distinct environment while providing collectors with exclusive access to fresh material.

This year's participants include ArtFactum/ Beirut presenting Marc Baroud & Marc Dibeh, Caroline Van Hoek/Brussels presenting Gijs Bakker, Elisabetta Cipriani/ London presenting Carlos Cruz-Diez, Industry Gallery/Washington DC & Los Angeles presenting Benjamin Rollins Caldwell, Volume Gallery/Chicago presenting Jonathan Muecke and Wonderglass/London presenting Nao Tamura.

In addition to the gallery and On/Site exhibitions, Design Miami/offers a diverse program of Satellites, Collaborations, a new Commission and Talks. As a Satellite Exhibition, Louis Vuitton premiers the first prototype of *La Maison au bord de l'eau*, designed by Charlotte Perriand in 1934 but never before realized. *Four (4): New Visions for Living in Miami* curated by Terence Riley invited Ateliers Jean Nouvel, Christian de Portzamparc, Diller Scofidio + Renfro and OMA (Office for Metropolitan Architecture/Rem Koolhaas) to design innovative solutions for residential living. The Cooper-Hewitt National Design Museum and ARTBOOK | D.A.P. collaborate to present a pop-up shop of designed objects and publications reflecting designers and architects represented in the fair's exhibition program. And Artsy again shares the fair's program with the global community online through presentations of work from each participating gallery, editorial from curators and critics and tours of the fair with collectors and specialists.

The 2013 Design Talks, presented by The Surf Club, continue to explore compelling topics in the design world. Three headline talks feature design luminaries who have shaped the American home. Architect Richard Meier reveals his thoughts about American Modernism, Margaret Russell, Architectural Digest's Editor-in-Chief, asks a designer from the AD100 list about integrating collectible design into the home, and Stefano Tonchi, Editor-in-Chief of W Magazine speaks with Martha Stewart about democratizing design.

Finally, Design Miami/ would not be possible without the generous support of our partners. This December, the fair's primary supporters will launch an impressive selection of designed installations commissioned specially for Design Miami/.

Exclusive Automotive Sponsor Audi celebrates its dedication to design with their site-specific installation *Fragmentation*. In addition, Audi organizes a VIP Car Service in the progressively luxurious Audi A8. Main Sponsor Swarovski Crystal Palace premiers *Mangue Groove* by Guilherme Torres, a designed environment of innovative led-free crystal and reclaimed wood that celebrates Miami's native mangrove forests. This year, long-term partner Fendi will continue its ongoing support of contemporary design and present the Design Collaboration *Metamorphosis*, an installation of new work by Maria Pergay. Exclusive Champagne Sponsor Perrier-Jouët returns to Miami with Dutch designer Simon Heidjens' *Phare n°1-9*, a design experience that reinterprets the maison's Art Nouveau history, propelling it into the twenty-first century. Design Miami's Collectors Lounge, designed by Cassina, will welcome guests to a sophisticated catered environment.

Our ninth fair in Miami presents the most international selection to date of exhibitions and designers, featuring twentieth century masters alongside the freshest faces of design. The increasing quality of gallery shows and compelling cultural programming creates a sense of maturity and excitement for the rich offerings in the field of collectible design.

We hope you enjoy Design Miami/2013!

Design Galleries/

Antonella Villanova/
Florence

Rike Bartels
Jamie Bennett
Manfred Bischoff
Helen Britton
Matteo Casalegno
Hugh Findletar
Lucia Massei
Jacqueline Ryan
Betty Woodman

For Design Miami/2013 Antonella Villanova focuses on a selection of innovative jewelry by Jacqueline Ryan, Helen Britton, Manfred Bischoff, Rike Bartels, Jamie Bennett and Lucia Massei.

Apart from these works, other objects promote the successful collaboration between designers and master craftsmen. The gallery presents a series of vases designed by Hugh Findletar called *Flower Heads*. These vases were made in Murano and blown by Oscar Zanetti, one of the most famous master glaziers in the world. Also on display is an appliqué by Betty Woodman in crystal and aluminium previously shown at the Museum of Fine Arts in Boston, and a bookcase *Volumi Sospesi* made of glass and ancient oak by Italian architect Matteo Casalegno.

Contact/Antonella Villanova
Address/Piazza Goldoni, 2 Palazzo Ricasoli, Florence 50123, Italy
Call/+390556802066
Email/antonellavillanova@gmail.com
antonellavillanova.com

Untitled/ Jacqueline Ryan, 2009
Gold, enamel / 55 x 60 x 22 cm
Courtesy of Jacqueline Ryan

PinkVoid / Johanna Grawunder, 2013
Anodized aluminum, LEDs, acrylic diffuser, colored gel / 83.8 x 83.8 x 65.5 cm
Courtesy of Carpenters Workshop Gallery

Carpenters Workshop Gallery/ Paris & London

Maarten Baas
Humberto & Fernando Campana
Johanna Grawunder
Random International
Robert Stadler

Carpenters Workshop Gallery, with spaces in both Paris and London, is the go-to destination for exclusive, limited-edition, contemporary design-art. Straddling the border between form and function since its inception, the gallery's international presence promotes an exciting line-up of established design masters alongside more emerging talent. With a full program of gallery shows and nine international art fairs this year alone, Carpenters Workshop Gallery provides an unrivalled platform for its artists to showcase their unique and limited-edition artwork to the industry and the wider public interest.

The gallery has cultivated strong relationships with the artists it works with and alongside those featured at Design Miami/, it also presents work by Atelier Van Lieshout, Sebastian Brajkovic, Andrea Branzi, Wendell Castle, Ingrid Donat, Vincent Dubourg, Lonneke Gordijn & Ralph Nauta, Mathieu Lehanneur, Frederik Molenschot, Nendo, Rick Owens, Pablo Reinoso and Charles Trevelyan.

Contact/Aurelie Julien
Address/54, rue de la Verrerie, Paris 75004, France
Call/+33142788092
Email/aurelie@carpentersworkshopgallery.com
carpentersworkshopgallery.com

PinkVoid/ *detail*

Casati Gallery/
Chicago

Franco Albini
Pietro Chiesa
Luigi Caccia Dominioni
Ignazio Gardella
Johanna Grawunder
Max Ingrand
Larry Lasky
Jonathan Nesci
David Salkin
Gino Sarfatti

For Design Miami/2013, Casati Gallery presents *REFLECTION on Post-War Italian Design*, an exhibition revealing a selection of historically important decorative art and furniture pieces in a booth designed specially by Jonathan Nesci. Works presented include a collection of distinct ceramics by Fausto Melotti, a selection of unique and rare furniture pieces by Franco Albini and rare lamps by Gino Sarfatti for Arteluce.

In addition Casati Gallery presents an extensive collection of vintage mirrors designed by Pietro Chiesa and Max Ingrand for Luigi Fontana/Fontana Arte and contemporary mirrors designed by Jonathan Nesci, Larry Lasky, David Salkin and Johanna Grawunder.

As part of its mission to promote Italian design, Casati Gallery presents the most recent publication on the work by Gino Sarfatti – *Gino Sarfatti: Selected Works 1938-1973* by Marco Romanelli and Sandra Severi Sarfatti.

Contact/Ugo Alfano Casati
Address/949 W. Fulton Street, Chicago IL, 60607, USA
Call/+13124219905, +13125936006
Email/info@casatigallery.com
casatigallery.com

Stadera desk, Luisa armchair & table lamp Mod. 539/ Franco Albini & Gino Sarfatti, 1958/1959/1955
Walnut, enameled steel, rosewood upholstery, enameled aluminum, vinyl/Various
Courtesy of Casati Gallery

Cristina Grajales Gallery/
New York

Sam Baron
Pedro Barrail
Rama Chorpash
Luigi Colani
Christophe Côme
Sebastian Errazuriz
Hechizoo
James Salaiz
Sèvres
Suzanne Tick

Since its inception in 2001, Cristina Grajales Gallery has established itself as one of the forerunners in the design world. The gallery specializes in contemporary design, while also dealing in masterpieces of the twentieth century.

Cristina Grajales Gallery focuses on cultivating the work of emerging designers who work in a variety of areas within the larger field of design: furniture and lighting, as well as ceramic, metal and textile design. Their work constantly pushes, blurs and in some cases erases the line between art and design.

With twenty years of experience, Grajales has established herself as a tastemaker and trendsetter both in contemporary and twentieth century design. Founded in 2001, Grajales' lecture series titled *Dialogues with Design Legends* at the 92nd street Y was the first of its kind. Grajales, widely considered an expert within the design field, is a frequent guest lecturer, panelist and contributor to various publications.

Cristina Grajales Gallery maintains a full program of exhibitions. The gallery also offers advisory and design consultancy services to assist in building and maintaining important collections.

Contact/Cristina Grajales & Lindsay Johnson
Address/10 Greene Street, 4th Floor, New York 10013, USA
Call/+12122199941
Email/info@cristinagrajalesinc.com
cristinagrajalesinc.com

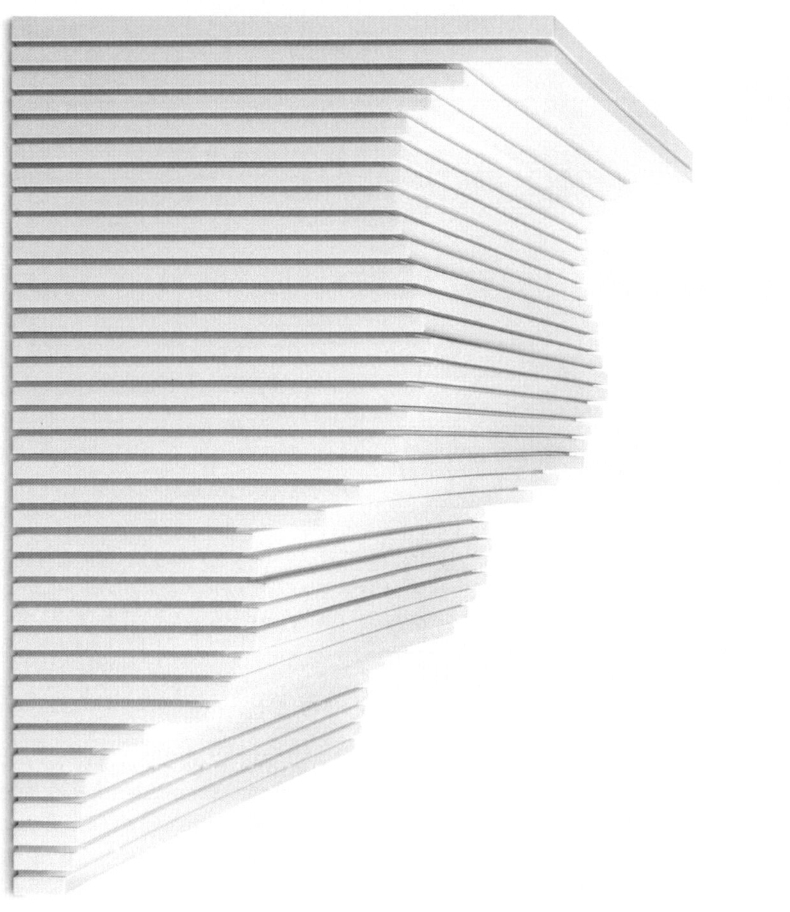

Molding Console/ Sam Baron, 2013
Lacquered wood/ 150 x 45 x 70 cm
Courtesy of Cristina Grajales Gallery

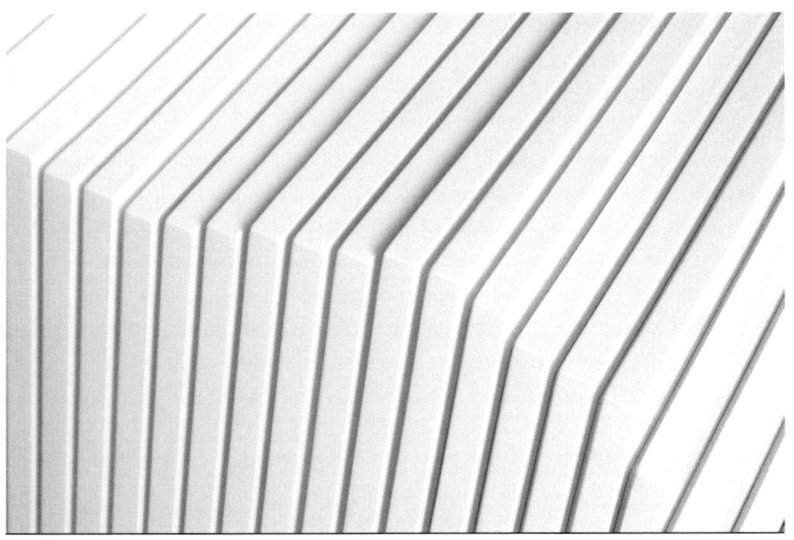

Molding Console/ *detail*

Demisch Danant/
New York

Maria Pergay
Sheila Hicks

Demisch Danant specializes in twentieth-century European design with an emphasis on the late 1950s through the 1980s. The gallery features the work of Maria Pergay, Pierre Paulin, Joseph Andre Motte, Pierre Guariche, Philippon & Lecoq, René Jean Caillette and Pentagon Group. The gallery also engages in a series of exhibitions concerning the intersection of architecture, design and art.

For Design Miami/2013, Demisch Danant presents a solo exhibition on renowned French designer Maria Pergay, accompanied by early works from Sheila Hicks. The exhibition includes a selection of Pergay's most iconic works of the 1970s presented in a Parisian-style living environment.

In 1968, Maria Pergay presented her first collection of stainless steel furniture at Galerie Maison et Jardin, under the direction of decorator Jean Dive. This seminal exhibition established Maria Pergay as one of the most innovative French furniture designers of her time and her work established stainless steel as a principal component of furniture design during the 1970s. Throughout the decade, Pergay collaborated with major manufacturers and worked on significant commissions for Pierre Cardin, The World Trade Center in Brussels and the Royal Family of Saudi Arabia among other esteemed clients.

After studying fine art at Yale under the tutelage of Josef Albers, Sheila Hicks established herself as one of the most innovative textile artists of the 20th century. Hicks is renowned for her painterly approach to textile design and an ability to craft environments through the unlikely medium of fiber. She has collaborated with prominent architects including Luis Barragán, Ricardo Legorreta and SOM. Her work defies categorization, simultaneously addressing several related mediums including painting, sculpture, design and installation.

Contact/Suzanne Demisch & Stephane Danant
Address/542 West 22nd Street, New York 10011, USA
Call/+12129895750
Email/info@demischdanant.com
demischdanant.com

Wave Desk *exhibited at Galerie Maison et Jardin, Paris, May 1968/* Maria Pergay, 1968
Stainless steel with leather insert/ 74 x 200 x 45 cm
Courtesy of Michel Nahmias

Didier Ltd/
London

Hans Appenzeller
Cesar Baldaccini
Pol Bury
Alexander Calder
Marisol Escobar
Marion Herbst
Ibram Lassaw
Roy Lichtenstein
Miye Matsukata
Robert Lee Morris
Louise Nevelson
Alicia Penalba
Lucio Del Pezzo
Pablo Picasso
Arnaldo & Gio Pomodoro
Edival Ramosa
Niki de St Phalle
Jesus Raphael Soto
Carol Summers
Jack Youngerman

Didier Ltd is a London-based gallery run by Didier and Martine Haspeslagh that specializes in jewelry by leading Modern Masters, painters and sculptors who are recognized internationally for their art. These jewels are historical pieces, conceived during the artists' lifetime and produced primarily from 1940 to 1990. As jewelry these pieces blur the boundaries between art and design, while also being small, intimate expressions of their creator's art.

For Design Miami/2013, Didier Ltd celebrates the fortieth anniversary of the groundbreaking exhibition *Jewelry as Sculpture as Jewelry* held in the Institute of Contemporary Art, Boston in 1973. The exhibition brought together 131 jewels by fifty artists or designers, many of whom were at the beginning of their careers. The gallery is fortunate to present at Design Miami/several unique pieces that were shown in Boston, as well as other works by those represented. The gallery is also producing an accompanying catalogue with photographs of the pieces worn by models, as in the exhibition's original purple-covered catalogue, which incorporated many photographs by Italian photographer Ugo Mulas that also appeared in contemporary issues of Vogue.

Contact/Didier & Martine Haspeslagh
Address/66b Kensington Church Street, London W8 4BY, UK
Call/+447973800415
Email/info@didierltd.com
didierltd.com

Large Kinetic Earrings / Jesus Raphael Soto, 1968
Silver, silver-gilt / 7 x 7 cm
Courtesy of Didier Ltd

Erastudio Apartment-Gallery/ Milan

Mario Bellini
Anne Bianchet
Gunjan Gupta
Jonathan De Pas, Donato D'Urbino and Paolo Lomazzi
Gaetano Pesce
Ettore Sottsass

Erastudio Apartment-Gallery was born in 2010 from the experience and professionalism of architect Patrizia Tenti, founder of the gallery.

The philosophy of Erastudio – "design as architecture" – transpires from the structure of its two spaces in the historical building of Via Palermo 5 in Milan. The gallery offices are located in an apartment on the third floor while the gallery itself is located in the "ex former stables" in the courtyard of the building. Each space is restored according to the concept "less is more". The name "Erastudio Apartment" recalls the influences of a past atmosphere where the "design works" are contextualized.

The gallery focuses exclusively on unique pieces, prototypes, artist's proofs, limited editions and special projects exclusively for its clients from Italian and international architecture and historical masters like Ettore Sottsass Jr., Carlo Scarpa, Mario Bellini, Napoleone Martinuzzi, Piero Fornasetti and Osvaldo Borsani as well as young designers. Erastudio works in between architecture and site-specific design providing consultancy and assistance to the adaptation and interaction of the pieces in a particular environment.

This has given rise to unique collaborations with artists/architects such as Gaetano Pesce (presenting America Table at Design Miami/2012 as a tribute to the American presidential election) Vincenzo De Cotiis and designers such as Indian Gunjan Gupta for the realization of special projects designed exclusively for the gallery. Among this path the concept of "design work" approaches the concept of "art work".

Since 2012 Erastudio has been accredited in the best fairs in the world of collectible design.

Contact/Patrizia Tenti
Address/Via Palermo no. 5, Ground floor/Courtyard & 3rd floor, Milan 20121, Italy
Call/+390239198515
Email/patrizia.tenti@erastudio.it & apartmentgallery@erastudio.it
erastudio.it

Matka Chair/ Gunjan Gupta, 2013
Brass, steel, aluminium / 81 x 76 x 160 cm
Courtesy of Erastudio Apartment-Gallery/Gunjan Gupta

Art Deco Centrepieces / Cardeilhac, 1930
Silver, marble, mirror / Centrepiece 17.5 x 33 x 12.5 cm, Mirror 57 x 32 x 3 cm,
Pair of small centrepieces 18 x 18 x 12 cm
Courtesy of Fine Art Silver

Fine Art Silver –
Francis Janssens van der Maelen/
Brussels

Maison Cardeilhac
Jean Després
Tété Knecht
Nicolas Le Moigne
Jean Puiforcat
Ettore Sottsass
Thalen & Thalen

Fine Art Silver is a Belgian gallery founded in 1978 by dealer Francis Janssens van der Maelen and is based in the buzzing Sablon neighborhood in Brussels.

Fine Art Silver has established itself as one of Europe's leading galleries in antique and modern silver objects and art works. Recently, the gallery has begun exhibiting contemporary silver design and presents new pieces edited for the gallery by European designers at Design Miami/2013.

The gallery has promoted contemporary silver design by editing and representing talents such as Thalen & Talen, Neda El'Asmar, Nicolas Lemoigne, Tété Knecht and Piet Hein Eek.

Contact/Francis Janssens van der Maelen
Address/Rue Ernest Allard 23, Grand Sablon, Brussels 1000, Belgium
Call/+3225027180
Email/jvdm@fineartsilver.com
fineartsilver.com

Pair of Candlesticks/ Jean Després, 1937
Silver-plated / 12.5 x 17.5 cm
Courtesy of Fine Art Silver

Gabrielle Ammann//Gallery/ Cologne

Nucleo
Florian Borkenhagen
Satyendra Pakhalé

One of the foremost contemporary design galleries in Europe, gabrielle ammann//gallery presents its exceptional program at Design Miami/2013 for the second time.

With over twenty years of experience curating exhibitions and initiating projects, Gabrielle Ammann has collaborated with the most significant figures in architecture and design including Ron Arad, Marc Newson and Zaha Hadid. In 2006, she established a permanent gallery space to create a forum to explore the intersection between architecture, fine art and design. The gallery exhibits iconic works by important designers as well as cultivates the best emerging designers of the twenty-first century.

Addressing the individual needs of clients, gabrielle ammann// gallery offers a range of services including acquisitions, collection management and curatorial work. With extensive interior design experience, Gabrielle Ammann provides consultation for both private and public spaces creating sophisticated environments by ingeniously integrating art and design. Working directly with important artists and designers, the gallery presents the opportunity to commission unique works of art and design for collections.

Contact/Gabrielle Ammann
Address/Teutoburger Strasse 27, Cologne 50678, Germany
Call/+492219328803
Email/contact@ammann-gallery.com
ammann-gallery.com

'Bronze Age' Coffee Table 01/ Nucleo, 2013
Polished Bronze, burnished bronze/120 x 80 x 36 cm
Courtesy of Nucleo Studio

Galerie BSL –
Béatrice Saint-Laurent/Paris

Djim Berger
Nacho Carbonell
Taher Chemirik
Charlotte Cornaton
Ayala Serfaty
Faye Toogood

Here Comes The Sun! is the theme chosen by Galerie BSL
for Design Miami/2013. A booth which mirrors a Miami
beach, with a cabana, a 1960s white American lounge chair
and a sandy beach hosting a colorful collection of works
explore the shifting boundaries between art and design,
sculpture and function, tradition and innovation.

In sunny yellow, blue and pink tones, intangible luminous
sculptures reminiscent of refined biomorphic forms by Israeli
designer Ayala Serfaty are presented, whose work is included
in the Metropolitan and the New York Museum of Arts and
Design collections.

A sunny yet intriguing atmosphere includes: a giant lamp
resembling a sea anemone and zoomorphic spider clocks
in bronze and agate stones by Nacho Carbonell, Designer
of the Future at Design Miami/Basel in 2009; a bench and
colorful stools including models for children resembling coral
or sponge, where porcelain is sensually renewed by Dutch
designer Djim Berger; an eighty-three inch high floor lamp
and throne-seat in a minimalist spirit by British designer
Faye Toogood; ceramic and glass vases and sculptures which
look like natural crystals by twenty-six year-old French visual
artist Charlotte Cornaton; new "Interior Treasures" pieces
by renowned jewelry designer Taher Chemirik, such as a
brass 'vegetation' screen; a low table including a seventy-one
inch massive rock crystal; and a carnivorous floor lamp
including rare hard stones.

Commissioned for Design Miami/, these unique or limited-
edition pieces each seek a new approach to the object.

Contact/Béatrice Saint-Laurent
Address/23 rue Charlot, Paris, 75003, France
Call/+33607454252
Email/bsaintlaurent@galeriebsl.com
galeriebsl.com

Mystic Garden/ Taher Chemirik, 2013
Brass / 350 x 60 x 240 cm
Courtesy of Galerie BSL – Béatrice Saint-Laurent

Galerie Downtown – François Laffanour/ Paris

Ron Arad
Choi Byung Hoon
Pierre Jeanneret
Charlotte Perriand
Jean Prouvé

When François Laffanour opened Galerie Downtown on the rue de Seine in 1982, he showed the work of Jean Royère, Mathieu Matégot, Charles and Ray Eames and George Nelson. He swiftly realized that the importance of the work of Le Corbusier, Jean Prouvé, Charlotte Perriand and Pierre Jeanneret also had to be recognized along with an in-depth examination of their careers.

These fascinating figures thought and created as architects, designers, craftspeople and industrial manufacturers. At one time overlooked, their rediscovery is largely due to the patient but unflagging work of Laffanour, whose reputation has henceforth been associated with architects' furniture.

He managed to acquire the archives of the Steph Simon Gallery, which produced and sold the works of Jean Prouvé and Charlotte Perriand between 1956 and 1974, and was an invaluable source of information. Just like the Steph Simon Gallery, Galerie Downtown exhibited Serge Mouille's lights and Georges Jouve's ceramics, which provide a powerful accompaniment to furniture.

Keen to spread the word about creative figures he admires, Laffanour was the first person in France to show Charles and Ray Eames, Mathieu Matégot, George Nakashima, George Nelson, Isamu Nogushi, Jean Prouvé, Charlotte Perriand and Jean Royère .

A gesture, a thought, a creative sensibility, a certain poetry, a spirit of their time - all help to explain the choices made by Laffanour with regard to the works of Ettore Sottsass, George Nakashima, Takis and Choï, whom he also exhibits, along with architect and designer Ron Arad, who has been represented by Galerie Downtown since 1994.

Contact/François Laffanour
Address/18 & 33 rue de Seine, Paris 75006, France
Call/+33146338241
Email/contact@galeriedowntown.com
galeriedowntown.com

Bookcase/ Charlotte Perriand, 1966
White tinted wood, braided rush, three lights integrated / 270 x 280 x 35 cm
Courtesy of Marie Clérin

Galerie Jacques Lacoste/
Paris

Georges Jouve
Alexandre Noll
Jean Royère

Specializing in twentieth-century decorative arts, Jacques Lacoste has set out to promote French design of the 1930s and 1950s.

Very passionate about 1950s decorative arts, Jacques Lacoste exhibits lighting by Serge Mouille, sculptures by Alexandre Noll and ceramics by Georges Jouve, Elisabeth Joulia, Pierre Szekely, Valentine Schlegel and André Borderie.

In February 2008, Lacoste opened a new gallery at 12 Rue de Seine with an exhibition of works by French sculptor Alexandre Noll. In September 2009 the gallery organized the first retrospective exhibition on glassmaker and designer Max Ingrand and contributed to the publication of his monograph *Max Ingrand: du verre à la lumière* by Pierre-Emmanuel Martin-Vivier (editions Norma, September 2009).

Particularly sensitive to the work and the universe of Jean Royère, Jacques Lacoste acquired the designer's archives in 1997 and dedicated two exhibitions to him in his Parisian gallery in 1999 and 2003 and in New York at the Sonnabend Gallery in collaboration with Galerie Patrick Seguin in 2008.

In 2003 he brought his expertise to bear on the publication of a book on Royère, *Jean Royère*, by Pierre-Emmanuel Martin-Vivier (Editions Norma, Paris).

His latest publication *Jean Royère*, in association with Galerie Patrick Seguin, is a two-volume boxed set gathering the numerous models and pieces Jean Royère designed, enriched with archival documents never shared before.

Contact/Jacques Lacoste
Address/12 rue de Seine, Paris 75006, France
Call/+33140204182
Email/lacoste.jacques@wanadoo.fr
jacqueslacoste.com

Low Ambassador Armchair/ Jean Royère, ca. 1950
Oak, velvet / 277 x 80 x 104 cm
Courtesy of Hervé Lewandowski

Ondulation Sideboard/ Jean Royère, ca. 1950
Ash, blue opaline glass / 230 x 45 x 89 cm
Courtesy of Hervé Lewandowski

MAKOTO (truth)/ Studio Wieki Somers, 2013
Anodized aluminum, LED, brass / 110 x 49.5 x 207 cm
Courtesy of Fabrice Gousset

Galerie kreo/
Paris

Ronan & Erwan Bouroullec
Jean-Baptiste Fastrez
Hella Jongerius
Gino Sarfatti
Wieki Somers

At Galerie kreo, Clémence and Didier Krzentowski produce and present limited-edition pieces by the greatest contemporary designers, such as Ronan & Erwan Bouroullec, Pierre Charpin, Naoto Fukasawa, Konstantin Grcic, Hella Jongerius, Alessandro Mendini, Jasper Morrison, Marc Newson, Martin Szekely, Studio Wieki Somers and others.

Limited-edition pieces produced for Galerie kreo are part of the permanent collections of the most important private collections and museums around the world.

Parallel to championing contemporary design, Galerie kreo also offers rare and exceptional vintage lamps, from the 1950s to the present day, with a focus on the Italian avant-garde, including masterpieces by Gino Sarfatti. Didier Krzentowski is indeed passionate about lighting and has been collecting for 30 years. The book published by JRP Ringier on his collection *The Complete Designers Lights* is considered a reference for vintage lights.

Didier Krzentowski is a licensed expert in design and contemporary art and is a member of the Union Française des Experts and Assesseur de la Commission de Conciliation et d'Expertise Douanière.

Contact/Clémence & Didier Krzentowski
Address/31 rue Dauphine, Paris 75006, France
Call/+33153102300
Email/info@galeriekreo.com
galeriekreo.com

Desk Light/ Ronan & Erwan Bouroullec, 2013
Lacquer, LED/37.5 x 26 x 29 cm
Courtesy of Fabrice Gousset

Galerie Maria Wettergren/ Paris

Mathias Bengtsson
Rasmus Fenhann
Enrico & Stine GamFratesi
Ditte Hammerstroem
Astrid Krogh
Eske Rex
Grethe Soerensen
Ilkka Suppanen

Galerie Maria Wettergren specializes in contemporary Scandinavian design and art. The gallery permanently presents and produces unique and limited-edition works by some of Scandinavia's leading designers such as Mathias Bengtsson, Astrid Krogh, Louise Campbell, Ditte Hammerstroem, Grethe Soerensen, Eske Rex, Rasmus Fenhann, Jakob Joergensen, Line Depping, Ilkka Suppanen, Mikko Paakkanen, Erling Christoffersen, GamFratesi, Niels Hvass, Hans Sandgren Jakobsen and Tora Urup. Several of these designers are represented in important museum collections such as the Centre Pompidou, the MoMA, the Cooper-Hewitt National Design Museum, the Contemporary Arts Museum in Houston and the Indianapolis Museum of Art.

The main interest of the gallery is the interdisciplinary dialogue between design, art and architecture. New ideas, technologies and materials are combined with the Scandinavian tradition of excellent craftsmanship, giving rise to sculptural and poetic objects and installations.

Maria Wettergren also organizes exhibitions by modern and contemporary photographers such as Rodolphe Proverbio and Etienne Bertrand Weill.

Contact/Maria Wettergren
Address/18 rue Guénégaud, Paris 75006, France
Call/+33677632881
Email/info@mariawettergren.com
mariawettergren.com

Suspended Plate/ Ilkka Suppanen, 2012
Murano glass, monofilament / 70 x 70 x 15 cm
Courtesy of Ilkka Suppanen

Reunited/ Ilkka Suppanen, 2012
Murano glass / 70 x 70 x 15 cm
Courtesy of Ilkka Suppanen

Galerie Patrick Seguin/ Paris

Le Corbusier
Pierre Jeanneret
Charlotte Perriand
Jean Prouvé
Jean Royère

Settled since 1989 in a gallery of three hundred square meters designed by Ateliers Jean Nouvel, Galerie Patrick Seguin promotes French creators such as Jean Prouvé, Charlotte Perriand, Pierre Jeanneret, Le Corbusier and Jean Royère throughout the world. Today, these designers are recognized as major contributors to the history of design in the twentieth century.

More recently, Patrick Seguin presented an entirely new scale of Prouvé's work with his most innovating dismountable architecture. This exhibition policy is backed by monographic or thematic publications.

This year, Galerie Patrick Seguin wishes to emphasize the scope of Jean Prouvé's genius, presenting for the first time at Design Miami/ 2013 a dismountable architecture.

The Maison 8x8, designed by Jean Prouvé in 1945, encapsulated perfectly Pouvé's notion of the mass-produced detached house – durable, light, economical and comfortable.

Contact/Patrick Seguin
Address/5 rue des Taillandiers, Paris 75011, France
Call/+33147003235
Email/info@patrickseguin.com
patrickseguin.com

Maison 8x8/ Jean Prouvé, 1945
Wood, metal/800 x 800 x 350 cm
Courtesy of Patrick Seguin

Maison 8x8/ Jean Prouvé, 1945
Wood, metal/800 x 800 x 350 cm
Courtesy of Patrick Seguin

Galleria Rossana Orlandi/ Milan

BCXSY
Nacho Carbonell
Enrico Marone Cinzano
Yukiko Nagai
Eiri Ota
Wonmin Park
Nika Zupanc

Galleria Rossana Orlandi opened in 2008 beside the Spazio Rossana Orlandi (2002) in Milan to create a specific platform for experimental and avant-garde design. Since the beginning, the gallery has focused on promoting and commercializing the works of young and upcoming designers from all over the world.

Contact/Marco Tabasso
Address/Via Matteo Bandello 14, Milan 20123, Italy
Call/+39024674471
Email/marco.tabasso@rossanaorlandi.com
rossanaorlandi.com

Peacock Chair/ Eiri Ota, 2013
Corian / 275 x 80 x 182 cm
Courtesy of Marco Tabasso

Gallery SEOMI/
Seoul & Los Angeles

Sehwa Bae
Jongsun Bahk
Byunghoon Choi
Jin Jang
Myungsun Kang
Sanghoon Kim
Hunchung Lee

Bringing contemporary design movements within one frame, Gallery SEOMI introduces contemporary design works that reflect the new constructionism and new organicism of Korea. The newly created works show a refined and eclectic vision, and have become new modern classics within their own culture. The works include those of Korean designers Bahk Jongsun, Bae Sehwa, Jang Jin, Kang Myungsun, Kim Sanghoon, Choi Byunghoon and Lee Hunchung. Suggesting a new paradigm of constructionism and organicism, they are both devoted to the idea of craftsmanship and to maintaining an originality that goes beyond contemporary ideas of form and style. They present dynamic yet understated design objects that represent the essence of modern life.

To enhance the aesthetic of modern Asian organicism with a considered approach to function, the recent versions of works, meticulously hand-made, possess their own context and reveal a unique design. They become iconic works and reflect modern ideas toward the principle and philosophy of craftsmanship and architectural naturalism. Beyond beauty, they are focused on new forms of structure and utility that rediscover the diverse style of living culture. As showcasing the interaction between the realm of design, art and architecture, they suggest new ideas and perspectives of the culture within integrated boundaries.

Contact/Lia Moon
Address/Chungdamdong 9-2, Gangnam, Seoul 135-100, Korea/
9038 Wonderland Park Avenue, Los Angeles, 90046, CA, USA
Call/+821095457916
Email/lia@seomituus.com
galleryseomi.com

afterimage 013-393/ Byunghoon Choi, 2013
White marble, Ipe / 176 x 80 x 30 cm
Courtesy of Gallery SEOMI

Trans-13-002/ Jongsun Bahk, 2013
Cherry, maple, walnut / 320 x 40 x 187 cm
Courtesy of Gallery SEOMI

Heritage Gallery/
Moscow

Nikolay Lansere

'Heritage International Art Gallery has been working on the Russian art market for more than six years. The gallery's name reflects the key goals that were set at its creation – its main function is to return the part of the Russian cultural heritage that has been lost. In 2011 'Heritage opened a new interiors and applied arts department, called 'Heritage Interior Art.

The gallery holds two major exhibitions a year. It presents new and revives often-forgotten facets of Russian art. One of the significant projects that attracted attention of collectors was the exhibition '*Heritage-Interior-Art: Dialectics of Interiors.* For the first time in Russia, the private gallery showed an exhibition of furniture masterpieces from the twentieth through twenty-first centuries.

'Heritage International Art-Gallery presents design projects devoted to the aesthetic of Soviet Art Deco style. It was one of the leading trends in all kinds of art of the Soviet Union from the mid 1930s to the mid 1950s. Its style combines the elements of Baroque, Napoleon Empire, late classical and Art D combination of luxury and monumentality.

The history of its origin is connected to the glorification of imperial power. It replaced the avant-garde and became the main style and aesthetic concept of the Soviet Union. It symbolized beauty, power and an ideal of government.

In 1936-37 there was a project to 'modernize' the interiors of the Marble Palace in St. Petersburg – it was to be adapted to the needs of the V. I. Lenin Museum, which had taken on this unique eighteenth century building. The updated interiors, including director's offices, were done as a project by Nikolay Lansere and D. A. Vasilev in the Special Technical Design Bureau, which also employed architects working on state orders for elite interiors, including Moscow's Kremlin. Nikolay Lansere came from the famous artistic family of Benua-Lansere.

Contact/Christina Krasnyanskaya
Address/20/1 Petrovka, Moscow 127051, Russia
Call/+74956250228
Email/gallery@heritage-gallery.ru
heritage-gallery.ru

Stools/ Nikolay Lansere, ca. 1930
Wood, linen/60 x 60 x 49 cm
Courtesy of Heritage Gallery

Hostler Burrows/
New York

Richard Filipowski
Berndt Friberg
Hans Hedberg
Finn Juhl
Wilhelm Kåge
Barbro Nilsson

Kim Hostler and Juliet Burrows founded
their New York gallery in 1998 and have
consistently led the evolving market of
Nordic design, championing and promoting
the work of Scandinavia's most prominent
designers of the twentieth century. The
gallery focuses on exceptional and unique
examples of studio ceramics, cabinetmaker
furniture and hand woven textiles by the
master artisans and architects of the period.

In March of 2013 the gallery reopened in its
new space at 51 East 10th Street, in the heart
of one of New York's richest destinations
for design and decorative arts.

Contact/Kim Hostler
Address/51 East 10th St, New York, NY 10003, USA
Call/+12123430471
Email/info@hostlerburrows.com
hostlerburrows.com

General Wolfe/ Richard Filipowski, 1960-1965
Phosphur bronze, silver/20 x 20 x 234 cm
Courtesy of Hostler Burrows

Cabinet/ Finn Juhl, 1950
Teak, brass / 78 x 48 x 81 cm
Courtesy of Hostler Burrows

Jason Jacques Inc/
New York

Amphora
Thorvald Bindesboll
Rene Buthaud
Jean Carries
Edouard Cazaux
Ernest Chaplet
Galileo Chini
T.A.C. Colenbrander
Paul Dachsel
Albert Louis Dammouse
Emile Decoeur
Taxile Doat
Christoper Dresser
Michael Geertsen
Georges Hoetnschel
Raoul Lachenal
Max Laeuger
Lucien Levy-Dhurmer
Louis Majorelle
Gareth Mason
Clement Massier
Abbe Pierre Pacton
Axel Salto
Eric Serritella
Ernst Wahliss
Vilmos Zsolnay

Red Horror/ Morten Løbner Espersen, 2013
Stoneware/135 x 107 cm
Courtesy of Jason Jacques Inc.

Jason Jacques Gallery holds the world's finest and most comprehensive collection of 1870-1920 European Art Pottery. Specializing in the Art Pottery Renaissance centered in 1890's France, the gallery's collection includes Art Nouveau and Japoniste masterworks by stoneware artists Ernest Chaplet, Jean Carries, Edmond Lachenal and Adrien Dalpayrat, in addition to the vast holdings of iridescent lusterware artists Lucien Lévy-Dhurmer, Clément Massier and Vilmos Zsolnay. In addition to the comprehensive collection of nineteenth century European Art Pottery, the gallery also represents innovative contemporary ceramic artists, including Michael Geertsen, Mason Gareth, Morten Lobner Espersen, Eric Serritella and Kim Simonsson.

Contact/Jason Jacques
Address/29 East 73rd Street #1, New York, NY 10021, USA
Call/+12125357500
Email/jason@jasonjacques.com
jasonjacques.com

Charred Heart, Sensual Vase & Vipers Nest/ Alphonse Voisin-Delacroix, Pierre-Adrien Dalpayrat & Maurice Gensoli,
1893–1930
Stoneware/Various
Courtesy of Jason Jacques Inc.

Table, Wall-lamp, Door/ Pierre Jeanneret, Serge Mouille, Jean Prouvé, 1954, 1957
Teak, metal, brass, painted aluminium/102 x 183 x 71 cm, 135 x 96 x 105 cm
Courtesy of Jousse Entreprise & Adrien Dirand

Jousse Entreprise/ Paris

Le Corbusier
Emmanuel Boos
André Borderie
Pierre Jeanneret
Georges Jouve
Kristin McKirdy
Mathieu Matégot
Serge Mouille
Pierre Paulin
Maria Pergay
Charlotte Perriand
Jean Prouvé
Jean Royère
Roger Tallon

For more than thirty years, Philippe Jousse has contributed to the growing recognition of designers such as Jean Prouvé, Charlotte Perriand, Le Corbusier, Pierre Jeanneret, Georges Jouve, Mathieu Matégot, André Borderie, Alexandre Noll, Serge Mouille and Jean Royére – all innovators of design in their time.

Jousse Entreprise comprises two galleries: one located at 18 rue de Seine in the sixth arrondissement of Paris dedicated to furniture from the 1950s and also from the 1970s; the space at 6 rue Saint-Claude is dedicated to contemporary art.

Contact/Philippe Jousse
Address/18 rue de Seine, Paris 75006, France
Call/+33153821360
Email/infos@jousse-entreprise.com
jousse-entreprise.com

Table, Chaise/ Pierre Paulin, 1968, 1972
Glass. aluminium, metal, tissue/72 x 120 x 60 cm, 76 x 52 x 52 cm
Courtesy of Jousse Entreprise & Adrien Dirand

Louisa Guinness Gallery/ London

Alexander Calder
William Ehrlich
Anish Kapoor
Jeff Koons
Claude Lalanne
Mariko Mori
Tim Noble & Sue Webster
Marc Quinn
Man Ray
Ed Ruscha
Conrad Shawcross
Frank Stella
Sophia Vari
Rob Wynne

This year Louisa Guinness Gallery celebrates 10 years of collaborating with artists to make jewelry.

The gallery opened in 2003 with its inaugural exhibition of artist's jewelry *Past and Present: Jewellery by Twentieth Century Artists.* This show placed specially-commissioned works by contemporary artists Antony Gormley, Ron Arad, Anish Kapoor, Ettore Sostass and Sam Taylor Wood beside the creations of Calder, Braque, Fontana and Niki de Saint Phalle.

Since then the gallery has collaborated with sixteen contemporary artists including Conrad Shawcross, Mariko Mori, Gavin Turk, Yinka Shonibare, Gary Hume and Tim Noble and Sue Webster to create jewels. At the same time it has built-up an impressive collection of historic jewelry, including pieces by Max Ernst, Pablo Picasso, Man Ray, Pol Bury and Fausto Melotti.

As the leading gallery in its field, Louisa Guinness Gallery works to the highest standard. All works are made by hand either in London's famous Hatton Garden, or in the artist's studio, and each piece is signed and numbered. At once jewelry and mini-sculpture, each piece holds an important place in the artists' wider body of work.

Contact/Louisa Guinness
Address/45 Conduit Street, London W1S 2YN, UK
Call/+442074944664
Email/info@louisaguinnessgallery.com
Louisaguinnessgallery.com

Untitled/ Pol Bury, 1968
Gold/ø7.2 cm
Courtesy of Louisa Guinness Gallery

Untitled Brooch/ Alexander Calder, 1940
Silver/ 11.5 x 5.5 cm
Courtesy of Louisa Guinness Gallery

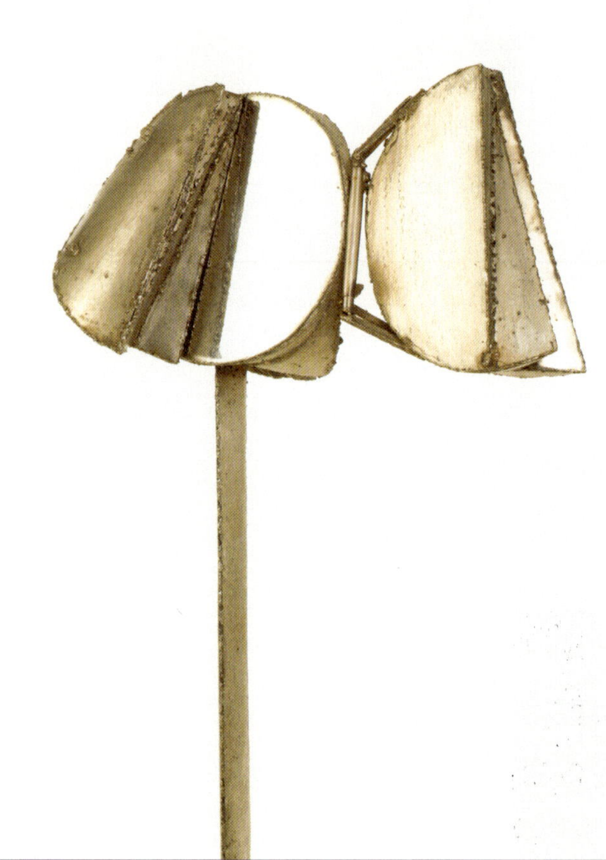

Sculpture Psyché/ *detail*

Magen H Gallery/ New York

La Borne
André Borderie
Agustin Cárdenas
Jim Cole
Le Corbusier
Georges Jouve
Gérard Mannoni
Marino Di Teana
Alain Douillard
Charlotte Perriand
Jean Prouvé
Jean Royère
François Stahly
Pierre Székely
Philolaos Tloupas

Since 1997, Magen H. Gallery has exhibited significant design in sculpture, decorative arts, architecture and ceramics with special emphasis given to French post-war design. Establishing greater visibility and appreciation for important works previously limited in reception, the curated collection emphasizes craft and concept exempt from ephemeral trends. Synthesizing modern and mid-century designers, the collection displays works that transcend form and function.

Contact/Hugues Magen & Nathalie Dheedene
Address/54 East 11th Street, New York 10003, USA
Call/+12127778670
Email/gallery@magenxxcentury.com
magenxxcentury.com

Sculpture Psyché/ Philolaos Tloupas, 1963
Stainless steel / 25.5 x 147 cm
Courtesy of Magen H Gallery

Mark McDonald/ Hudson

Walter Lamb
Art Smith

Mark McDonald Gallery is the latest exhibition space for Mark McDonald, a preeminent dealer in mid-twentieth century decorative arts, including furniture designed by architects such as Frank Lloyd Wright, Gerrit Rietveld, Alvar Aalto and Frank Gehry.

McDonald's expertise in the field is the result of three decades of experience, organizing landmark exhibitions on Frank Lloyd Wright, Charles and Ray Eames, Art Smith and the Studio Jewelry Movement, Nordic Design, American Studio Ceramics and Abstract Expressionists. He began in New York City in 1982 at his groundbreaking Fifty/50 Gallery in Greenwich Village. In 1995 he moved to Manhattan's Meatpacking District on Gansevoort Street. And in 2002, McDonald embarked on a new venture, moving north to the Hudson Valley.

McDonald's current gallery is housed in a renovated, historic, three-story building that was originally built as a department store in 1910. The first floor houses furniture, textiles, books, ceramics and lighting, and features jewelry by Alexander Calder, Harry Bertoia, Margaret De Patta, Art Smith and Claire Falkenstein. Currently, the second floor is used for gallery exhibitions and the third houses offices and a research library.

Mark McDonald and the gallery are perhaps best known for assembling and advising important collectors and museums: Vitra Design Museum, Los Angeles County Museum of Art, Montreal Museum of Decorative Arts, The Daphne Farago Jewelry Collection (recently given to the Museum of Fine Arts, Boston), the John Waddell *American Modern* exhibition at The Metropolitan Museum of Art and the Art Smith *Village to Vogue* exhibit at The Brooklyn Museum.

Contact/Mark McDonald
Address/555 Warren Street, Hudson, NY 12534, USA
Call/+15188289282
Email/330@markmcdonald.biz
markmcdonald.biz

Outdoor Rocker & "Patina" Necklace/ Walter Lamb & Art Smith, ca. 1950
Bronze, rope, brass/Various
Courtesy of Mark McDonald

MFA Boston Bench/ David Ebner, 1995
Bronze / 91.5 x 39 x 43 cm
Courtesy of Moderne Gallery

Moderne Gallery/ Philadelphia

Arthur Espenet Carpenter
Wendell Castle
David Ebner
Wharton Esherick
Sam Maloof
George Nakashima
Toshiko Takaezu
Peter Voulkos

Founded in 1984 by Robert Aibel, Moderne Gallery
is an internationally recognized gallery for 20th century
decorative arts - with a primary specialization in work
from the American Craft and Studio Movement, 1925-1990.
It includes a large collection of work by Wharton Esherick,
George Nakashima, Sam Maloof, Arthur Espenet
Carpenter, Wendell Castle, David Ebner, Peter Voulkos,
Paul Soldner, Edward Moulthrop, James Prestini and
most of the major figures of the movement.

Contact/Bob & Josh Aibel
Address/111 N. 3rd Street, Philadelphia, PA 19106, USA
Call/+12159238536
Email/info@modernegallery.com
modernegallery.com

Ornamentum/
Hudson

David Bielander
David Clarke
Iris Eichenberg
Karl Fritsch
Ted Noten
Ruudt Peters
Gerd Rothmann
Philip Sajet
Petra Zimmermann

Ornamentum is thrilled to exhibit special presentations of works by Iris Eichenberg and Karl Fritsch at Design Miami/2013.

German born artist-designer Iris Eichenberg contemplates the absence of image in her latest body of work X. Nail-heads covering the surface like scales or the bubbled skin of electro-formed iron give texture and depth, hinting to the faint form of eye-sockets and a chin - the memory of facial features lost in the fog of time embodied in both wearable and art objects and sculptures in the vaguely recognizable form of the human head.

Iris Eichenberg currently holds the title of Head of the Metalsmithing Department at the prestigious Cranbrook Academy of Art, after years of teaching at the Gerrit Rietveld Academy in Amsterdam.

Possibly the world's most playfully irreverent studio jeweler working today, German-born, New Zealand-based Karl Fritsch simultaneously discards and embraces the historical foundations of jewelry making and design. Whether it is modeling a precious gold ring as if by a child, or setting gemstones with a screw or a bent carpenters nail, Fritsch's attitude of setting his own rules has garnered a following among art and jewelry collectors worldwide. A special selection of (mostly) rings spanning two decades in this designer's oeuvre will be exhibited at Design Miami/2013.

Founded in 2002, Ornamentum Gallery exhibits a dynamic collection of contemporary jewelry as well as related objects and artworks. Ornamentum hosts numerous exhibitions yearly in one of the world's largest gallery spaces dedicated specifically to contemporary jewelry and artworks where featured designer-artists display their work in conceptual installations.

Contact/Stefan Friedemann
Address/506 Warren Street, Hudson, NY 12534, USA
Call/+15186716770
Email/info@ornamentumgallery.com
ornamentumgallery.com

From the Series X: Necklace and Object/ Iris Eichenberg, 2013
Steel, electroformed pure iron, mirrored perspex / 38 x 38 x 27 cm
Courtesy of Tim Thayer

Untitled/ Magdalene Odundo, 2013
Ceramic / 28 x 28 x 58 cm
Courtesy of Pierre Marie Giraud

Pierre Marie Giraud/
Brussels

Morten Løbner Espersen
Fukumoto Fuku
Jean Girel
Valerie Hermans
Takuro Kuwata
Kristin McKirdy
Tony Marsh
Ritsue Mishima
Jin Morigami
Ron Nagle
Barbara Nanning
Magdalene Odundo
Tadanori Okazaki
Rick Owens
Nadia Pasquer
Sterling Ruby
Alev Ebbüzziya Siesbye
Bente Skjottgaard
Kazuo Taklguchl
Shouchiku Tanabe
Akiyama Yo
Kimura Yoshiro

Specializing in contemporary decorative arts, Pierre Marie Giraud represents international artists working with glass, ceramics and silver, and collaborates with designers for the production of unique objects and limited editions. A rich selection of modern and contemporary pieces makes the gallery's ceramics program particularly noteworthy.

Pierre Marie Giraud represents the best among African, European, North American and Japanese artists, and regularly features solo or thematic exhibitions of their work. The gallery issues publications about the artists featured in its exhibitions, collaborates with multiple museums on the promotion of modern and contemporary ceramics and participates frequently in international fairs.

Contact/Pierre Marie Giraud
Address/7 rue de Praetere, Bruxelles 1050, Belgium
Call/+3225030351
Email/info@pierremariegiraud.com
pierremariegiraud.com

Priveekollektie Contemporary Art|Design/ Heusden aan de Maas

Reinier Bosch
Dominic Harris
De Intuïtiefabriek
Arik Levy
Ifeanyi Oganwu
Roderick Vos

Priveekollektie represents internationally recognized artists and designers and provides young and upcoming talents with a platform for showing their exceptional collectible design and art pieces. Key in the collection is the combination of contemporary art and limited-edition design and the crossing of the fine line between both disciplines.

Before opening the gallery in 2006, Irving and Miriam van Dijk avidly collected art and design. Their personal approach, knowledge and taste have developed one of the leading galleries for collectible design in Europe, with exceptional exhibitions and participation in renowned international fairs for both contemporary art and design.

Contact/Irving & Miriam van Dijk
Address/Pelsestraat 13, Heusden aan de Maas, 5256AT, The Netherlands
Call/+31416858424
Email/gallery@priveekollektie.com
priveekollektie.com

Whaam! / Reinier Bosch, 2013
Glass, RVS bronze mirror, Plexiglas, LED lighting / 130 x 130 x 38 cm
Courtesy of Carolina Wilcke & Rachel Nieborg

Unique Accretion Vase/ The Haas Brothers, 2013
Hand-thrown ceramic with porcelain slip / 49.5 x 9.5 cm
Courtesy of Sherry Griffin

R 20th Century/
New York

The Haas Brothers
Hugo França
Joaquim Tenreiro
David Wiseman
Jeff Zimmerman

R 20th Century is a New York
based gallery representing
historical and contemporary
design from the United States,
South America, Europe and Asia.

Founded in 1997 by Zesty Meyers
and Evan Snyderman, the Tribeca
gallery runs an exhibition program
with the goal of promoting a closer
study, appreciation and preservation
of twentieth and twenty-first
century design.

R 20th Century specializes in
unique and rare vintage works by
designers including Wendell Castle,
Greta Magnusson Grossman, Poul
Kjærholm, Verner Panton, Sergio
Rodrigues, Joaquim Tenreiro
and Jose Zanine, to name a few.

The gallery also represents
contemporary designers Hugo
França, Hun-Chung Lee, Renate
Müller, Christian Wassmann,
The Haas Brothers, David Wiseman
and Jeff Zimmerman.

Contact/Zesty Meyers & Evan Synderman
Address/82 Franklin Street, NY 10013, USA
Call/+12123437979
Email/r@r20thcentury.com
r20thcentury.com

Sebastian + Barquet/
New York

Fontana Arte
Carlo Bugatti
Franco Campo & Carlo Graffi
Pierluigi Giordani
Piero Fornasetti
Ico Parisi

Sebastian + Barquet was founded in 2005 by Ramis Barquet. Sebastian + Barquet specializes in post-war, twentieth century American and Italian design and decorative art as well as selected work by contemporary designers. Emphasis is primarily on rare and important works by designers, artists and architects whose work has left an indelible mark on the design landscape.

Located in New York's premier arts district in Chelsea, at the historic Starrett-Lehigh building, the gallery's collection includes historic and iconic works by George Nakashima, Paul Evans, Harry Bertoia, Ico and Luisa Parisi, Gio Ponti and Carlo Mollino as well as contemporary pieces by Johnny Swing, Peter Macapia and Michael Coffey.

In addition to regular shows in the gallery space and a revolving inventory in its showroom the gallery participates in several design fairs per year around the globe.

Contact/Tara DeWitt
Address/601 W 26th Street, Ste 300, New York 10001, USA
Call/+12124882245
Email/info@sebastianbarquet.com
sebastianbarquet.com

Dining Table/ Franco Campo and Carlo Graffi, 1955
Mahogany, glass, chrome-plated metal/79 x 230 x 97 cm
Courtesy of Sebastian + Barquet

Lounge Chair/ Pierluigi Giordani, ca. 1958
Walnut, fabric, brass/59 x 73 x 83.8 cm
Courtesy of Sebastian + Barquet

Collection of Light, led 400/ Humans Since 1982, 2012
Wood, glass, LEDs/150 × 150 × 7 cm
Courtesy of Victor Hunt Designart Dealer

Victor Hunt
Designart Dealer/
Brussels

Tomas Alonso
Julien Carretero
Humans Since 1982
Jon Stam
Sylvain Willenz

We make and trade designart.

Victor Hunt Designart Dealer has curated contemporary design since 2008. The gallery's services focus on the development and production of limited editions by the most remarkable emerging designers.

We understand designart as the gray zone within industrial design, craft, architecture, sculpture and many other art disciplines. Victor Hunt is a branded personality of ourselves, an alter ego capable of customising our relation with each customer in constant personal progress. We offer the designs the industry can't.

Contact/Alexis Ryngaert
Address/Lambert Crickx 16,
Brussels 1070, Belgium
Call/+3227879957
Email/victor@victor-hunt.com
victor-hunt.com

Contrast, #3 - version 1/Julien Carretero, 2013
Stainless steel, copper, patina shade/145 × 95 × 16 cm
Courtesy of Victor Hunt Designart Dealer

Design On/Site Galleries/

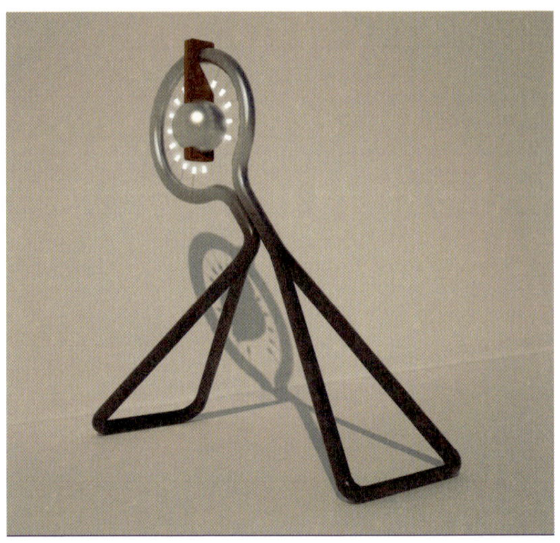

Desk Lamp/
Marc Baroud & Marc Dibeh, 2013
Steel, aluminum, oiled walnut/20 x 45 x 51 cm
Courtesy of Art Factum Gallery

Art Factum Gallery/
Beirut

Marc Baroud
Marc Dibeh

Art Factum Gallery is a fresh space devoted to presenting all forms of contemporary art and design. Founded in 2011, the gallery is located in Beirut's industrial Quarantine District, and exists as the renovated product of an old steel factory.

When dealing with contemporary art, and as an establishment that focuses on bringing in international artists to the cultural scene of Beirut, Art Factum Gallery manages to emphasize its presence and project it forward by applying to several international art fairs and events, while retaining a tight bond with several international galleries and institutions. That, along with collaborating with local cultural organizations and personnel, insures the subsequent spreading of the artistic message to the masses - one of the gallery's main motives.

As for the design scene, with the country's artistic spotlight having slightly shifted into the more utilitarian and three-dimensional aspect of art forms and products, Art Factum Gallery chooses to mostly endorse local designers. The gallery's specific annual design show serves to introduce new talents or propagate designers that have already launched their careers, all in all serving to emphasize the importance of contemporary Lebanese design. The designers and the gallery gravitates to using local materials and crafts for the production of the design work.

Art Factum Gallery represents and supports several international and local artists and designers in the Middle Eastern region.

Contact/Joy Mardini
Address/Rehban Street, Alley 204, Building 13, Medawar District, Quarantine, PO box 166271, Lebanon
Call/+9611443263
Email/contact@artfactumgallery.com
artfactumgallery.com

Lamp With Shelf/ Marc Baroud & Marc Dibeh, 2013
Steel, aluminum, oiled walnut / 44 x 31 x 170 cm
Courtesy of Art Factum Gallery

Caroline Van Hoek/ Brussels

Gijs Bakker

Caroline Van Hoek opened in 2007 to show jewelry, silver and related objects by contemporary international artists and important antique works.

Contact/Caroline Van Hoek
Address/Rue van Eyck 57, Brussels 1050, Belgium
Call/+3226444511
Email/info@carolinevanhoek.be
carolinevanhoek.be

Nadal Brooch/ Gijs Bakker, 2013
Gold on Titanium/10 x 7.4 x 0.18 cm
Courtesy of Gijs Bakker & Pauline Barendse

Bracelet "Holes"/ Gijs Bakker, 1992
Gold/Made to measure, 14.6 x 6.8 x 1.9 cm
Courtesy of Gijs Bakker

Chromointerférence/ Carlos Cruz-Diez, 2013
18kt white gold, rhodium plating, impresac acrylic with UV pigment / ø6 cm
Courtesy of Elisabetta Cipriani

Elisabetta Cipriani/
London

Carlos Cruz -Diez

Elisabetta Cipriani – Jewellery by Contemporary Artists is an invite to the most innovative and challenging living international sculptors and painters to create wearable sculptures with the use of precious metals and stones. It is the first time that these artists have approached jewellery establishing parallels with their artistic disciplines and poetics.

Carlos Cruz-Diez is internationally considered a master living artist of our time for his contributions to the theory and practice of color. Most recently in April 2012, he inaugurated a monumental artwork of architectural integration, consisting of walkways for the Miami Marlins ballpark.

For the Design On/Site program, Carlos Cruz-Diez strongly intervenes with the presentation of eleven pieces of jewelry, four of which were realized for the occasion of the fair and an op wall sticker specifically thought and designed for the booth. The focus of this representation is on color, line and the viewer's perception.

The jewelry pieces presented will be four bracelets, two necklaces, two rings and rare brooches that the artist had hand made in the 1970s for his family and friends. These pieces gather two types of self-defined op art categories: Physichoromies and Choromointerferences. All of his color-based experiments focus on variations of the observer's position in relation to the work, the light directed at the work, and the relationship between the colors presented.

The new pieces are made in 18kt yellow and white gold and realized in a limited edition of five to ten pieces.

Since 2009 the gallery has collaborated with: Atelier van Lieshout, Carlos Cruz-Diez, Enrico Castellani, Giorgio Vigna, Giuseppe Penone, Ilya & Emilia Kabakov, Jannis Kounellis, Kendell Geers, Massimiliano Fuksas & Mimmo Paladino, Rebecca Horn, Tatsuo Miyajima, Tom Sachs, Wim Delvoye and Erwin Wurm.

Contact/Elisabetta Cipriani
Address/At Sprovieri, 23 Heddon Street, London W1B 4BQ, UK
Call/+447981646790
Email/elisabetta@elisabettacipriani.com
elisabettacipriani.com

Binary Chair 02/ Benjamin Rollins Caldwell, 2013
Recycled computer parts, hardrives, disk drive / 104 x 63.5 x 46 cm
Courtesy of Industry Gallery

Industry Gallery/
Washington DC & Los Angeles

Benjamin Rollins Caldwell

Industry Gallery, the only US gallery focused exclusively on twenty-first century design, opened in January 2010 in Washington D.C. Occupying over 4000 square feet of space in a converted auto repair shop, the gallery holds temporary exhibitions of work by designers selected for their ability to illuminate a broad spectrum of international design.

As the name suggests, Industry Gallery presents designers who are creating new and innovative works with the use of modern industrial materials. These materials range from common items such as recycled magazine paper and glass to more sophisticated materials such as aluminum and carbon fiber.

The gallery's generous exhibition area allows each designer to tell his or her own story through site-specific installations designed to transform the perception of space. By loading the interior of the gallery with disparate items, each designer evokes complex and multiple associations to create a three-dimensional painting.

The gallery opened its second exhibition space in Los Angeles in March of 2011, in the historic Pacific Design Center, one of the West Coast's top design destinations and home to a branch of the Museum of Contemporary Art (MOCA).

Contact/Craig Appelbaum
Address/1358 Florida Avenue, NE, Suite 200, Washington DC 20002, USA
Call/ 1 12023991730
Email/craig@industrygallerydc.com
industrygallerydc.com

Binary Chair 01/ Benjamin Rollins Caldwell, 2013
Recycled computer parts, hardrives, disk drive/94 x 91 x 69 cm
Courtesy of Industry Gallery

Volume Gallery/ Chicago

Jonathan Muecke

Volume Gallery is a gallery with a specific focus on American design, and a strong emphasis placed on emerging contemporary designers. Volume Gallery releases editions, publications and organizes exhibitions that showcase the work of American designers to regional, national and international audiences. We are asking critical questions of what it means to be an American designer in a culture that is rapidly becoming more global, while simultaneously examining the American experience.

In Volume Gallery's second solo exhibition with Jonathan Muecke, he continues his exploration of OPEN OBJECTS across dominant typologies -table, light, bench, chair. "The periphery is the position that I prefer for my practice — it is ideologically free. I do not distinguish architecture from design. I am interested in interior and exterior — the interior of an object and the exterior of space."

Contact/Claire Warner & Sam Vinz
Address/845 W Washington Blvd, 3rd Floor, Chicago IL 60607, USA
Call/+13122248683
Email/claire@wvvolumes.com
wvvolumes.com

Painted Shape/Jonathan Muecke, 2013
Painted aluminum/65 x 26.5 cm
Courtesy of Volume Gallery

Stabilizer/ Jonathan Muecke, 2013
Carbon fiber/ 55 x 15 x 50 cm
Courtesy of Volume Gallery

Wonderglass Ltd/ London

Nao Tamura

The reflections of the Venetian cityscape glistening on the evening water hints at an imaginary city below the moving surface. There is a border between the world under and the land above. In the city of Venice, where the real world and fantasy coexists, this chandelier is the embodiment of the beauty of dual worlds.

Flow[T] is a contemporary chandelier inspired by the colors of the Venetian lagoon and customized to the desires of each owner. Each piece enjoys its own shape, and in multiples, they create a sculptural display of lighting.

For it's official launch in Milan Wonderglass drew upon the time-honoured experience of Venetian master glass-blowers and the contemporary touch offered by artists and designers of international renown, capable of interpreting the beauty of glass in a spectacular, innovative manner paired with the most advanced technological research on lighting. What we hope to do is encourage people to notice things that they no longer notice; to reach a sort of unconscious recognition that everyone instinctively feels and understands.

The nature of our products and the aim of our vision is to provide our customers with an effective degree of flexibility - we truly believe in the tailor-made blowing.

Contact/Maurizio L.M. Mussati
Address/7–10 Chandos St, London W1G 9DQ, UK
Call/+447595777924
Email/mmussati@wonder-glass.com
wonder-glass.com

Flow[T] / Nao Tamura, 2013
Blown glass / S3 ø9.8 x 97.1 cm, S4 ø24.9 x 42.4 cm, S2 ø9.9 x 88.1 cm
Courtesy of Light Emisson Direct

Special Programming
& Design Satellites/

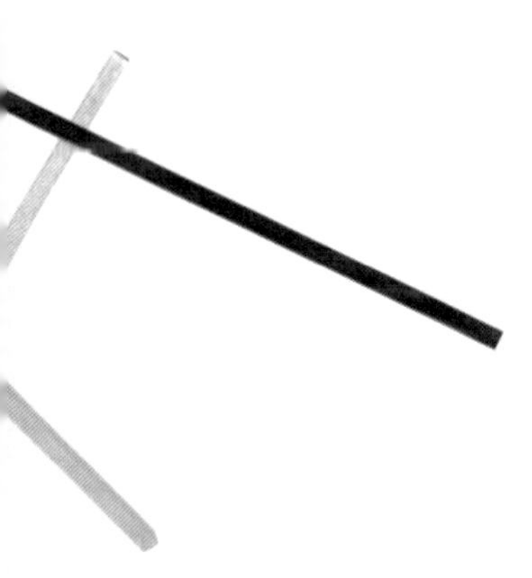

AUDI/

Designer Among Designers/

Audi has continuously shown its commitment to design and innovation through insightful commissions with designers and architects including Tom Dixon, Moritz Waldemeyer, Mirko Borsche, Bjarke Ingels, Clemens Weisshaar and Reed Kram.

Each of Audi's installations at the Design Miami/fairs have highlighted key elements of Audi's technological advancements and married automotive design with the most current developments in product, graphic, digital and set design, urban planning and architecture.

This December at Design Miami/2013, Audi creates the site specific installation *Fragmentation* focusing on Audi Sport. The red rhombus is THE symbol for high-performance and outstanding Audi technology in both series production and motorsport. At Design Miami/the Audi Sport emblem will be transformed in a three- dimensional installation. The spotlight will be on two extraordinary Audi models, the R8 Spyder, which is the top-sporting model of Audi and the R8 LMS ultra, which Audi offers for customer motorsport and has the same genes as the production model.

R8 LMS ultra
quattro GmbH
BILSTEIN
quattro GmbH
MICHELIN

Swarovski Crystal Palace presents/

Mangue Groove
by Guilherme Torres/

Premiering at Design Miami/2013, Swarovski Crystal Palace presents *Mangue Groove* by Guilherme Torres, an innovative architectural installation inspired by the Brazilian mangrove forests. Swarovski Crystal Palace supports emerging talent within the fields of art, architecture and design.

This collaboration evokes an ongoing mission of Swarovski to teach the importance of water conservation to children across the world. Water is a vital ingredient in the crystal making process and led to the creation of the Swarovski Waterschool in 1999. Currently active in many countries worldwide, the Swarovski Waterschool program will expand to Brazil in 2014.

Mangrove forests – mangue in Portuguese – have long been considered emblematic of Brazil's natural beauty and are essential in protecting Brazilian coastal environments. At the heart of his installation, Torres uses the mangrove forests as a symbol of the growing conservation surrounding the preservation of Brazil's endangered aquatic ecosystems.

Torres creates an installation that combines the natural beauty and function of the Mangrove forests with the structure and concept of the Voronoi diagram. The Voronoi diagram, the division of spaces into cells with corresponding focal points, acts as the DNA for the *Mangue Groove* installation.

Torres brings these concepts to life through his use of synthetic tubes filled with Swarovski's lead-free advanced crystals, linked together by geometric joints of certified and reclaimed wood. The installation will resemble a mangrove forest, while the wooden joints of the structure will be placed at intervals that will follow the outline of the naturally occurring Voronoi diagram. Visitors will be able to navigate through the space by walking on certified and reclaimed wooden pathways that will guide them in between the rising mangrove structures.

Mangue Groove will also experiment with the effects of light and sound to create an all-encompassing experience for the visitors. Each day at 5 pm, a dynamic mixture of light patterns and sound recordings will slowly build in movement and tempo, to mimic the views and sounds one might see and hear during an Amazonian sunset, a trademark beauty of the country.

SWAROVSKI CRYSTAL PALACE

Eduardo Banderas G/
americaelementall.com

Design Collaboration/
Maria Pergay for FENDI/

For the 2013 edition of Design Miami/, FENDI presents an installation derived from its ongoing collaboration with Maria Pergay. The presentation includes a distinguished and iconic environment with a series of exceptional pieces imagined by the designer.

Pergay humorously and skillfully combines warm and cold; fur and stainless steel; her universe with that of FENDI. This partnership highlights values which FENDI and Pergay share, such as excellence, boundless creativity, mastery of materials, savoir-faire, beautiful craftsmanship and a real passion and devotion to artisanship.

The idea behind the partnership is to highlight the bond between leather and fur workmanship, iconic FENDI materials and Pergay's stainless steel designs.

Pergay offers an interpretation of time passing and metamorphosis. Besides her technical performance, the designer evokes something much more subtle, which can be perceived in her creations – a fervor for life in a delicious revolt.

Since her debut, there has been a sense of peace and rebellion, of power and serenity, alongside a distinctive sense of humour, fantasy and the refusal to adhere to any stereotype. Her work also reveals a magnificent tribute to the natural world demonstrated through her use of furs created at FENDI's Fur Atelier in Rome.

Pergay also enjoys playing with trompe l'oeil effects and has commissioned special pelts inspired by marquetry and inlaid with different materials, paying tribute to what FENDI has designed, revisited and reinterpreted with extraordinary furs over the decades.

Fendi's commitment to experimentation is deeply routed in the company's culture. A proud partner of Design Miami/ since 2008, Fendi has been actively supporting contemporary design and craftsmanship through various creative collaborations with designers Aranda\Lasch, Moritz Waldemeyer, Elisa Strozyk, Formafantasma, Nacho Carbonell, Simon Hasan, Peter Marigold and Kwangho Lee, among others.

Pouf Goéland/ Maria Pergay for FENDI, 2013
Stainless steel and natural fox fur

Phare n°.1–9/ Simon Heijdens, 2013

Perrier-Jouët presents/

Phare nº. 1–9
by Simon Heijdens/

In celebration of beauty and infusing art into everyday life, Perrier-Jouët invited Simon Heijdens to create this year's Experience.

At the occasion of Design Miami/2013, Heijdens has created a unique experiential installation that reinterprets Art Nouveau, propelling it into the twenty-first century.

As Art Nouveau saw Jules Chéret introduce the printed poster, and Louis Lumiére create moving pictures, Heijdens now presents a new medium of expression that echoes the period's temperament of aesthetic innovation.

Reflecting on Perrier Jouët's own material essence, the work explores water as a dimensional volume, a translucent refracting medium for light, and finds a completely new way of drawing and building up images. A constantly evolving story grows within the water and is illuminated to fully immerse the space in pattern. The totally white environment that hosts this enchanting experience becomes the screen upon which one can both walk around and walk inside the narrative to experience it from different perspectives.

Simon Heijdens' works merge the allegorical and the tangible and explore the concept of coincidence to trace and reveal the hidden essence of the spaces and objects that surround us in everyday life. Founded in Rotterdam in 2002, his studio has been based in London since 2005.

Design Talks/

Presented by The Surf Club

Design Miami's Design Talks program presents the design world's most compelling current topics, bringing together the creatives, collectors and critics actively influencing design discourse and production. The 2013 Talks feature luminaries who have shaped the American home. Pritzker Prize-winning architect Richard Meier gives insight into his distinct American Modern style, Margaret Russell, Architectural Digest's Editor-in-Chief, discusses collecting and interiors with AD100 Designer Muriel Brandolini, and Stefano Tonchi, Editor-in-Chief of W Magazine speaks with Martha Stewart about her role in changing the way Americans live with design.

This December's Design Talks are presented by The Surf Club Hotel and Residences. Set on eight acres of pristine Atlantic oceanfront on Miami Beach, The Surf Club Hotel and Residences combine the elegant, purposeful architecture of Richard Meier with a unique provenance and history. Founded as a private social club in 1930, The Surf Club played an important role in the cultural history of Miami Beach as a nexus for the most exceptional personalities of the era, from scions of industrial fortunes to the Duke and Duchess of Windsor, Winston Churchill, Frank Sinatra and Elizabeth Taylor. The Surf Club Hotel and Residences present Meier's translation of The Surf Club's historical architecture into a luxurious compound comprising two twelve-story residential buildings, an intimate five-star hotel, two restaurants and sumptuous spa offering a broad spectrum of wellness, beauty and fitness experiences.

THE SURF CLUB

HOTEL & RESIDENCES

Wednesday, December 4, 6–7pm/
American Modernism
A conversation with Richard Meier

Thursday, December 5, 6–7pm/
Interiors, Art and Design
AD100 designer Muriel Brandolini
in conversation with Margaret Russell
Editor-in-Chief of Architectural Digest

Friday, December 6, 6-7pm/
Democratizing Design
Martha Stewart
in conversation with Stefano Tonchi

Margaret Russell/
Courtesy of Joshua McHugh

Stefano Tonchi/
Courtesy of Inez Lamsweerde
and Vinoodh Matadin

Martha Stewart/
Courtesy of Scott Duncan

Muriel Brandolini/
Courtesy of Charles Thompson

Richard Meier/
Courtesy of DBOX, 2013

Charlotte Perriand/ 1934
Courtesy of ACHP2013

Charlotte Perriand/
La Maison au bord de l'eau, 1934

Louis Vuitton Tribute/

Pursuing a collaboration based on a shared vision of women, Louis Vuitton is embarking on a new venture in the company of Charlotte Perriand.

Having designed the "Icons" collection inspired by Perriand's talent and lifestyle, Louis Vuitton is creating *La Maison au bord de l'eau* for Miami Art Week.

La Maison au bord de l'eau was designed by Charlotte Perriand in 1934. Internationally renowned for her pioneering designs, Charlotte Perriand also led the way in prefabricated holiday homes. She was incredibly passionate about this project, which was particularly important to her but was never actually realized. Destined for mass production, *La Maison au bord de l'eau* was aimed at a wide-ranging public as an ecological holiday residence, designed to be assembled and dismantled as required. Mounted on stilts, it could be sited in the middle of the countryside, or by the sea, a lake or river.

Eighty years after *La Maison au bord de l'eau* was conceived, Charlotte Perriand's daughter and Louis Vuitton have teamed up to build the first prototype of this house, which reflects a generous 1930s utopia that links social needs with architecture, prefabrication technologies and home furnishings. It is a rare example of modern architecture where a house has been designed to be at one with the interior scheme and the furniture.

La Maison au bord de l'eau has been constructed according to the original plans, under the guidance of Pernette Perriand-Barsac who worked as her mother's assistant for twenty-five years. The house is furnished, as Charlotte Perriand wished, with pieces she designed between 1929 and 1942 of which no original examples remain, only the drawings and photos in the archive. Each piece of furniture in the house is individually numbered and signed. Together, they form a unique heritage collection that respond brilliantly to the needs of contemporary living, a collection that has been revived thanks to Louis Vuitton.

LOUIS VUITTON

La Maison au bord de l'eau/ 1934
View from the terrace

La Maison au bord de l'eau/ 1934
Overhead view

*Four (4): New Visions
for Living in Miami/*

Curated by Terence Riley & Produced by David Martin, Terra Group/

Four (4): New Visions for Living in Miami originated as a challenge to a select group of leading architecture firms to come up with innovative visions for mid-rise residential living surrounded by the leafy green canopy of Coconut Grove, suspended between the blue skies above and the blue waters of Biscayne Bay below.

Miami-based developer Terra Group chose the architects – Ateliers Jean Nouvel, Christian de Portzamparc, Diller Scofidio + Renfro and OMA (Office for Metropolitan Architecture/ Rem Koolhaas). The curator and exhibition designer is Terence Riley, former director of the Miami Art Museum and former chief curator of Architecture and Design at the Museum of Modern Art.

In the exhibition, original drawings and models prepared by the architects are accompanied by text and additional materials that convey their visions. *Four (4)* offers viewers an in-depth understanding of the ways in which architects address the challenges and opportunities inherent in a mid-rise residential development that aspires to be an asset to the community and an urbanistic building block for the future.

Presented by the Terra Group and Related

Coconut Grove Project/ Diller, Scofidio + Renfro, Architects, 2013
Presentation Model/
Photography by Stephan Goettlicher

Homage to Charlotte Perriand/

Charlotte Perriand, a Modernist Pioneer, from Avant-garde Design to Photography/

A comprehensive exhibit which includes furnishings, fashion and photography

Louis Vuitton shares its passion with Cassina for Charlotte Perriand, one of the most intriguing and pioneering female icons from the twentieth century with a comprehensive exhibit that includes furnishings, fashion and photography.

Cassina, the only authorized company to manufacture the furniture designed by Charlotte Perriand, celebrates this exceptional collaboration with a preview of the travelling exhibition of the architect's photography at the Cassina Miami showroom during Design Miami/and Art Basel Miami Beach 2013. The photographic memories are an insight into her passion for architecture, natureand humanity discovered during her travels, all constant themes in her works. A selection of furniture designs by Perriand – manufactured by Cassina – will be displayed along with the photography exhibit.

An inspired installation in collaboration with Louis Vuitton will underline this Perriand homage.

Cassina will also participate in Louis Vuitton's authentic to-scale reconstruction of the *La Maison au bord de l'eau*, designed by Perriand in 1934, which will be on show in the spectacular setting of Miami Beach during Design Miami/ and Art Basel 2013.

December 5–16
Cassina Showroom at Poltrona Frau Group Miami
Address/3800 NE Miami Court, Miami Design District 33137
pfgmiami.net

Cassina

Grès sur le sable/ Charlotte Perriand, 1935
Courtesy of ACHP ADAGP 2013

Tokyo Outdoor/ Charlotte Perriand, 1940
Courtesy of Cassina

Courtesy of Matthew Sandager

ARTBOOK
& The Shop at Cooper-Hewitt/

International art and design book publisher and retailer
ARTBOOK | D.A.P. presents a curated selection of books
and objects in partnership with The Shop at Cooper-Hewitt,
National Design Museum.

ARTBOOK is pleased to offer the newest and best books on
twentieth-century and contemporary design from the world's
most important publishers, with a special focus on titles related
to Design Miami/exhibitors.

The Shop at Cooper-Hewitt presents a selection of objects by
established and emerging designers that will surprise, delight
and inspire. The product mix includes many exclusive items
that relate to both Design Miami/and the Museum's extensive
permanent collection.

Smithsonian
Cooper-Hewitt, National Design Museum

Artsy/

Artsy's mission is to make all the world's art accessible to anyone with an Internet connection. We are an online platform for discovering and collecting art and design. Our growing collection comprises 50,000+ works by 11,000+ artists from leading galleries, museums, foundations, and artists' estates.

Powered by The Art Genome Project – a way of providing pathways for discovery for experts and non-experts alike – Artsy hopes to foster new generations of art and design lovers, museum-goers, collectors, and patrons. We are honored to partner with 500+ leading galleries, as well as 140+ museums and foundations.

We're thrilled to once again partner with Design Miami/ to create an online experience that complements The Global Forum for Design. Users on Artsy.net and Artsy's iPhone app can browse and inquire about works from the fair, read exclusive editorial content, gain insight from industry insiders and acquire works for sale by fair exhibitors, opening up the Design Miami/ experience to our growing network of over 175,000 visitors around the world. For the first time in Miami, visitors to the fair can meet Artsy representatives in person and charge their mobile phones while checking out our site and app.

Contact/ Alex Gilbert
Email/ alex@artsy.net
artsy.net

ART.SY

Hall 1 Süd/ Herzog & de Meuron, 2013
Courtesy of Iwan Baan

Design Miami/

The 2013 Design Commission/ A discourse formed with Formlessfinder.

Each December, Design Miami/ commissions early-career architects to build a designed environment for the fair's entrance as part of its biannual Design Commissions program. New York-based architectural practice Formlessfinder are the designers of the 2013 pavilion, and here they talk about formless architecture, their practice and their Tent Pile project.

Designers in Charge/ Garrett Ricciardi, Julian Rose. Structural Engineer/ Robert Silman Associates, Nat Oppenheimer, Ben Rosenberg. Aluminum Fabrication/ Neal Feay Company, Alex Rasmussen. Environmental Engineering Consultation/ Mahadev Raman, Patrick Regan. Special Project Support provided by ALCOA. Images Courtesy of Formlessfinder, Neal Feay Company. Year/ 2013. Location/ Miami Beach, Florida. Area/ 2900 square feet. Weight/ 500 tons.

Formlessfinder's pavilion outside of Design Miami/

Formlessfinder's **Tent Pile** pavilion brings an intensely architectural intervention to **Design Miami/**, inventing a new building typology to provide shade, seating, cool air, and a space to play for the city's public. The design practice, co-founded by **Julian Rose** and **Garrett Ricciardi** in 2010, approaches new projects with an interest in the specifics of geography — closely examining the spatial, social, and physical conditions of the location with which their structure will interact. They prioritize the use of available materials, committing to deploy them in ways that allow for reuse, an approach that produces what they refer to as **"an architecture that can go from nothing to something and back again."**

"We call ourselves Formlessfinder in part because our studio operates as a 'finder' in the sense of an app or a search engine, something that can fluidly analyze a wide range of inputs and produce diverse outputs (buildings, pictures, videos, models, texts, products, information).

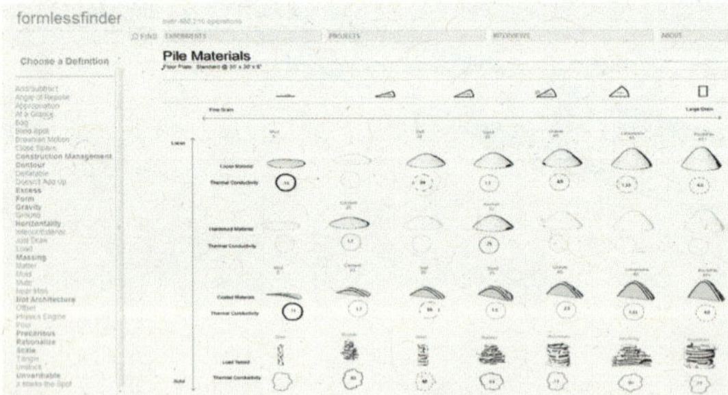

"Finding" pile materials Traditional distinctions between media disappear: a video might become a kind of drawing or a software program a way of constructing an argument. But across this range, our approach to the formless is always grounded in an exploration of the physical processes, materials, and structures that we see as the fundamental building blocks of architecture."

In researching ideas for this project, Rose and Ricciardi ultimately focused on two phenomena very particular to Miami. The first was the ubiquity of sand in the region;

Miami Beach the same material that has made the city's beaches famous also lies beneath the foundations of its buildings. Any kind of construction in Miami must take into account the loose and shifting layer on which the final structure will ultimately float.

This condition remains hidden below the surface of most Miami architecture, but Formlessfinder saw in it exciting possibilities: sand's weight might offer a counterintuitive stability and its very looseness could provide new flexibility in tectonics and construction,

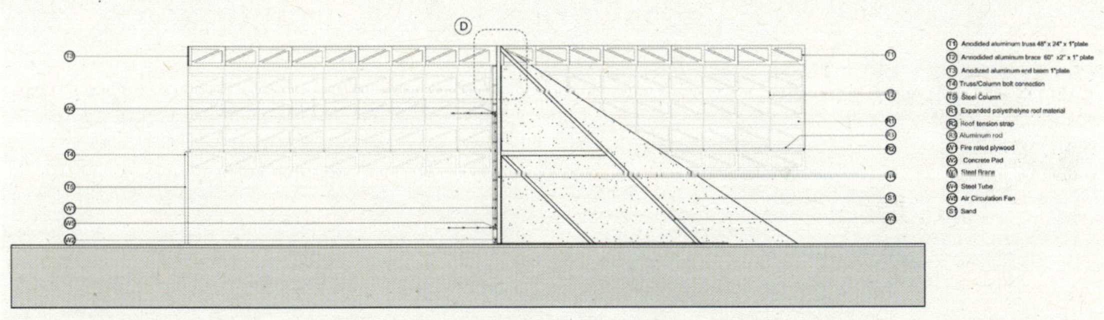

Longitudinal section of the pavilion while the aesthetic of the material itself could take on an iconic resonance in a region where neighbourhoods and cities are named after local beaches.

The second attribute of the city to catch Rose and Ricciardi's attention was its architectural vernacular. They were fascinated by a typology of public space that emerged from the collision of an exuberant post-war modernism with Miami's tropical climate: hybrid indoor/outdoor spaces that are sheltered by dramatically cantilevered roofs yet not enclosed by walls, inviting passerby to take refuge from sun or rain while also allowing free and fluid access to all. The challenge of mediating between the mass and looseness of sand and the lightness and precision of the cantilever was met through an innovative approach to structure and materials.

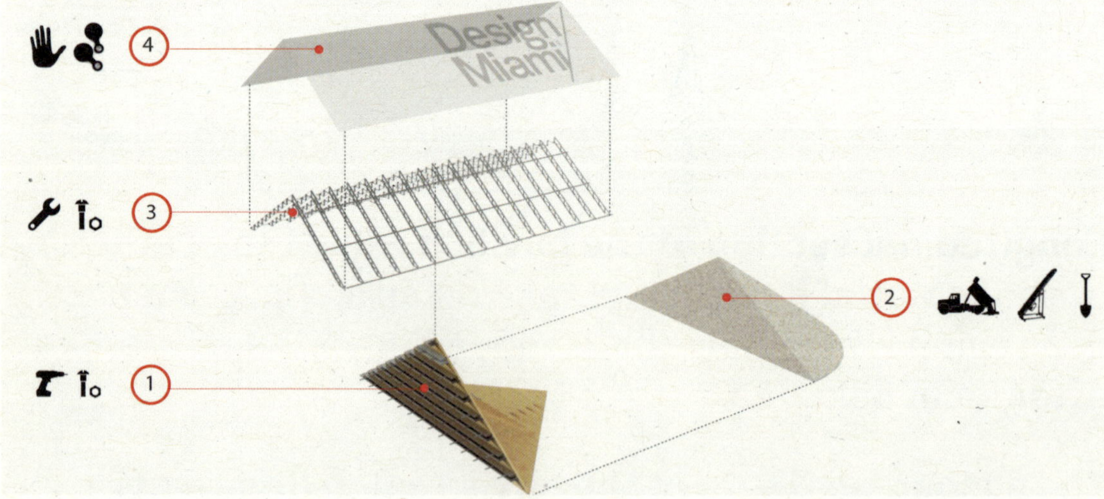

Aluminum truss production, Neal Feay
The sand that is so destabilizing for architectural projects elsewhere in Miami became the stabilizing element of Tent Pile, with a massive pile of the material — left loose and unaltered so that it would be completely reusable after its time on the site — acting as a ballast to stabilize a lightweight aluminum roof, in lieu of a traditional excavated foundation.

The four key elements of the pavilion construction

To increase the expanse of open space under the roof, Formlessfinder designed a retaining wall to slice the cone of sand in half, creating a more ordered space immediately in front of the entrance to the fair. Bench seating offers visitors a place to lounge,

Seating under the pavilion and the space is conditioned by a simple system that takes advantage of the thermal mass cooling effect of the huge pile — the steel superstructure bracing the retaining wall is embedded deep within the sand, and draws the cool temperatures of the pile's interior into the seating area, with fans creating a refreshing breeze rippling out from the wall.

Diagram of the cooling system

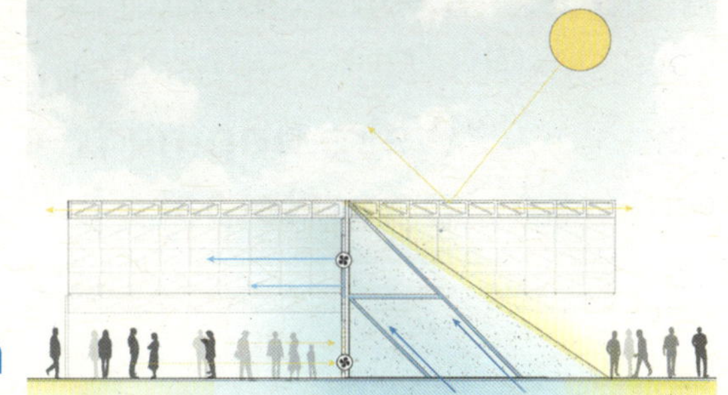

Tent Pile acts as a refuge for the more than 50,000 visitors who come to Miami for the fairs each year, as well as inhabitants of the city's South Beach neighborhood. It is intended as a new kind of public building that marries the practical requirements of shelter and seating to a radical re-envisioning of architecture's fundamental organization and operation.

"When you really think about it, there's almost no dimension of architecture that isn't inflected by form. Form has always been the public face of architecture: the side of itself the discipline most readily offers to the world. And formal systems — from the ancient orders to Renaissance theories of proportion to the parametric platforms of today — have typically controlled everything from architecture's cultural symbolism to its programmatic layout and tectonic organization. The danger of this arrangement is that architectural possibilities cease to exist outside formal possibilities;

even when people think they're talking about something else, like function or structure, there's often some kind of formal idea underlying the discussion...."

Yet even as Formlessfinder's project probes the limits of architecture itself, it remains literally grounded in materials and aesthetics specific to Miami, as well as celebrating the location of the fair within the city — the pyramid of sand is there to be sat on and played in, the cooling fans to be approached, examined and enjoyed. **"We're hoping to create something that people will want to participate in,"** says Ricciardi, and the result is a structure designed to be occupied and explored, as much as admired.

500 tons of Miami sand stabilize the roof

"...The formless subverts typical ways of thinking about and making architecture, but it is not actually foreign to the field because it is fundamentally about space and material. So the formless is not another symbolic attack on architecture; it's a de-idealization, a de-sanitization, and an opening up. It is messy. It's about getting things out of control, and uncovering some of the architectural depth that lies below form."

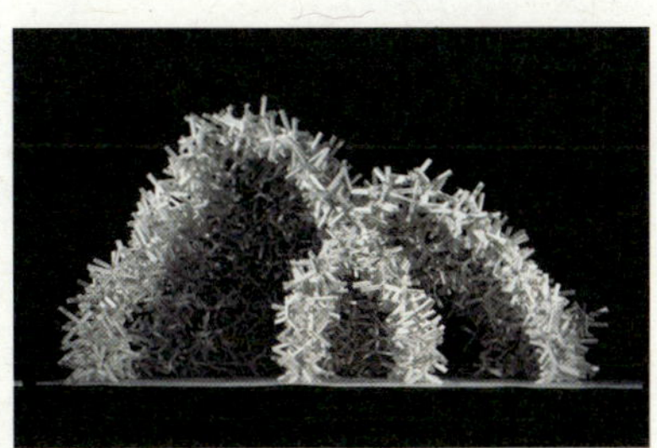

Burr is a brick that refuses to stack rationally because it has too many embedded possibilities. It can be used to construct the same archetypal structures expected of more traditional masonry units, using the same general principles of load bearing compression to form arches and domes. Its behavior is broadly predictable, staying within certain bounds of probability and structural behavior. But as burrs are stacked, they tangle and shift, inevitably corrupting any specific idealized configuration.

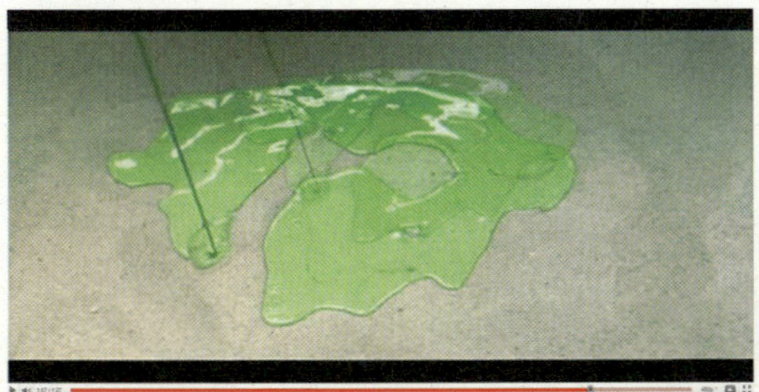

Ground co-opts a found topographic condition, transforming it into a roof canopy. Architects tend to sublimate ground as landscape, and so-called "landform" buildings produce ground as metaphor, looking like hills or mountains. Ground is ground. It is produced by a complete reversal of normal practices of creating space. Excavation replaces enclosure; pouring down replaces building up. Persistent and repeated inversions of solid and void, matter and space, and ground and air leave structure and space mutually destabilized.

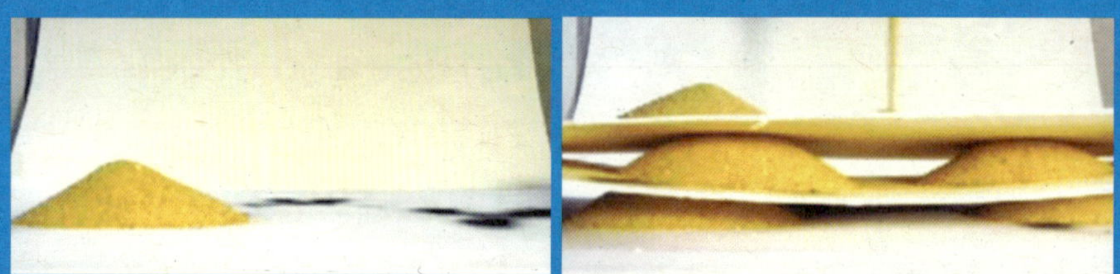

Load Test is a slab building predicated on the realization that anything can perform structurally. Here piles of raw matter replace columns. The age old drama between architecture and gravity is restaged, but tectonic form is no longer the triumphant hero. Instead, the piles achieve an ambiguous equilibrium. Neither vertical nor horizontal, they deny the expected identification between human body and vertical structural element.

http://www.Formlessfinder.com

Acknowledgements/

Design Miami/is made possible through the generous support of Dacra, a creative real estate company specializing in innovative projects combining architecture, art, design and fashion.

Design Miami/is partnered with MCH Group

Design Miami/wishes to express enthusiastic appreciation for our sponsors

Exclusive Automotive Sponsor/

Main Sponsor

Design Collaboration with Maria Pergay/

Exclusive Champagne Sponsor/

Design Talks Presenter /

Collectors Lounge Design/

Furniture Partners/

Cassina

Poltrona Frau

cappellini

Alias

Design Commission Supporters/

Online Partner/

Hospitality Partner/

Providers/

Museum Partners/

Smithsonian
Archives of American Art

Smithsonian
Cooper-Hewitt, National Design Museum

Design Miami/wishes to thank the Cities of Miami Beach and Basel and the local authorities for their support

www.basel.ch

Special Thanks/ René Kamm, CEO of MCH Group

Art Basel/ Marc Spiegler, Director/Annette Schönholzer, Director of New Initiatives/Magnus Renfrew, Director Asia/ Marco Fazzone, Director of Resources and Finance/ The Art Basel Team

Board of Directors/ René Kamm/Craig Robins

Executive Board/ Marianne Goebl/Thomas Hochuli/ René Kamm/Craig Robins/Annette Schönholzer/ Anna Williams

Gallery Committee/ Suzanne Demisch/ Pierre Marie Giraud/Clémence & Didier Krzentowski/ Laurence & Patrick Seguin

Vetting Committee/ Simon Andrews/Dr. Al Eiber/ François Laffanour/Alexander von Vegesack

City of Miami Beach Mayor/ Matti Herrera Bower

Vice Mayor/ Jonah Wolfson

City Manager/ Jimmy L. Morales

Assistant City Manager/ Jorge Gomez

Commissioners/ Jorge Exposito/Michael Gongora/ Jerry Libbin/Edward L. Tobin/Deede Weithorn

Department of Tourism and Cultural Development/ Max Sklar/Graham Winick/Linette Nodarse

City of Miami Beach Cultural Arts Council
City of Miami Beach Police Department
City of Miami Beach Fire Department

Acknowledgements with thanks/ Audra Asencio/ Princess Alia Al-Senussi/Bevin Bailis/Cub Barrett/ Marisa Batista/Caroline Baumann/Pietro Beccari/ Tracy Belcher/Charles Bell/Jean-Denis Benbassat/ Larissa Braun/Ibiayi Briggs/Giulio Capua/Carter Cleveland/ Isabel Chattas/Tiffany Chestler/Nicholas Christopher/ Katherine Cocke/Kiera Coffee/Thom Collins/Silvia Cubiña/ Sebastian Cwilich/Axelle de Buffévent/Luca de Meo/ Sarah Doyle/Wolfgang Egger/Aldo Faetti/Silvia Fendi/ Angella Forbes/Patrick Foret/Alexander Galan/ Alexandra Gilbert/Monica Gioia/Bob Goodman/ Mary Gomez/Elinor Groden/Philippe Guettat/ Marian Gulbrandsen/Austin Harrelson/Sarah Harrelson/ Kate Haw/Rory Hermelee/Mary Hoeveler/David Holtzman/ Mayda Horstmann/Sharon Hurowitz/Nicole Irizarry/ Anthony Ingham/Tali Jaffe/Paul James/Thomas Kaminski/ Samuel Keller/Virginia Klautau/Mateo Kries/Erik Larkee/ Amy Lau/Cathy Leff/Tara Levy/John Lin/ George Lindemann/Andrea Lipps/Rodrigo Londono/ Christy MacLear/Nadine Marti/Cara McCarty/ Richard Meier/Stéphanie Mingham/Cristiana Monfardini/ Nancy Murray/Bernhard Neumann/Sascha Nikitin/ Sandra Novas/Todd Oldham/Tommy Ralph Pace/ Brian Pendrack/Matthew Peschke/Ermanno Piraes/ William Pittell/Demetra J. Prattas/Meire Ramos/ Alex Rasmussen/Stefanie Reed/Katrin Regler/ Garrett Ricciardi/Emily Rom/Julian Rose/Cory Reynolds/ Megan Riley/Terry Riley/Maria Ruiz/Margaret Russell/ Trey Sarten/Jackie Sayet/Michael Schwartz/Melanie Seitz/ Emily Shattan/Aviva Shulem/Stefan Sielaff/Lucie Simon-Rehm/Yann Soenen/Maria Sole Henny/Julien Sovez/ Kathrin Speidel/Jessica Spirer/Rupert Stadler/ Leann Standish/Martha Stewart/Francis Sultana/ Nadja Swarovski/Michael Tiedy/Stefano Tonchi/ Mark Turkel/Corey Tuttle/Marc Zehntner/

Design Miami/ Organization

Principal/ Craig Robins

Chief Operating Officer/ Steven Gretenstein

Co-Founder/ Ambra Medda

Vice President/ Anna Williams

Director/ Marianne Goebl

Director of Marketing/ Kapila Chase

Director of Exhibitions/ Alexandra Cunningham

Logistics Director/ Ty Bassett

Sponsor & VIP Relations Manager/ Brittany Silver

Exhibition Manager/Brandon Grom

Operations Manager/ Joanne Greene

Logistics Manager/ Kevin Perkins

Operations Coordinator/ Bryan Mendez

Exhibition Architect/ Komal Kehar

Online Editor/ Rob Goyanes

General Counsel/ Linda Ebin/Patrick Graber

Director of Finance & Administration/ Jon Levin

Project Accounting/ Carrie Acosta/Marcia Katz/ Marisel Rodriguez

Sponsorship & Communications/ Ainsworth Associates/ Susan Ainsworth, President

Public Relations/ Camron PR/Judy Dobias, Managing Director/Adnan Abbasi/Valentina Giani/ Lisa Mcmillan/Sarah Natkins/Doug Roche/James Hart

Identity, Collateral & Signage/ Made Thought

Project Architects/ Aranda\Lasch

For the garage.
And the pit.
The Audi R8 LMS ultra.
For more information, visit www.audi-motorsport.com
R8 LMS ultra
Audi Sport
customer racing
V10
BILSTEIN
quattro GmbH
Exclusive Automotive Sponsor of Design Miami/

Audi Sport
Vorsprung durch Technik
MICHELIN

SWAROVSKIGROUP.COM
© 2013 D. Swarovski Distribution GmbH _ SWAROVSKI ®
SWAROVSKI
Proud to sponsor
Design Miami / 2013
designers' choice SINCE 1895

FENDI

“DRAWING LETS YOU EXPRESS THINGS IN A DIFFERENT WAY. YOU CAN BE SAD OR YOU CAN BE ROMANTIC. YOU CAN BE AN IDIOT. ANYTHING CAN WORK IN A DRAWING.”

RONAN BOUROULLEC

Disegno. Daily

disegnodaily.com

CHAMPAGNE
PERRIER-JOUËT

PERRIER-JOUËT, THE ALLURING CHAMPAGNE

Since its foundation in 1811, the champagne house Perrier-Jouët has crafted elegant, floral wines of rare finesse with a Chardonnay hallmark. The elegance of the cuvees echoes that of the Art Nouveau anemones adorning the Belle Epoque bottle and offers moments of pure delight and beauty. www.perrier-jouet.com. Please Enjoy Our Fine Wines Responsibly. PERRIER-JOUËT® PRODUCT OF FRANCE.
© 2013 PERNOD RICARD USA, PURCHASE NY

LOUIS VUITTON &

CHARLOTTE PERRIAND

ARCHITECTURAL DIGEST

ARCHDIGEST.COM

TUMBLR
archdigest.tumblr.com

TWITTER
@archdigest

FACEBOOK
facebook.com/architecturaldigest

INSTAGRAM
@archdigest

PINTEREST
pinterest.com/archdigest

THE SURF CLUB
HOTEL & RESIDENCES

Darling,

I must confess that I
have completely fallen
in love with this place
I cannot wait fo
your arrival!

YOY

9011 COLLINS AVENUE, SURFSIDE, FLORIDA 33154
THESURFCLUB.COM | P. 305.330.4000
Corcoran Sunshine Marketing Group, Exclusive Sales and Marketing Agent

THE SURF CLUB
HOTEL & RESIDENCES

cappellini
Alias
Cassina
Poltrona Frau
Fondata nel 1912
Poltrona Frau Group Miami is a proud sponsor of Design Miami/ 2013
3800 NE Miami Court | Miami Design District, FL 33137
305.576.3636 | www.poltronafraumiami.net

The only authorized authentic
Cassina is a proud sponsor of Design Miami/2103
Cassina
"LC3 Outdoor" by Le Corbusier, Jeanneret, Perriand and Cassina. Design first.
"One of the greatest joys for the human spirit lies in the perception of natural order" (P. Jeanneret). The new LC Outdoor collection withstands the harshest climates. Through careful research and experimentation with the finest and most innovative materials all LC Outdoor models are fit for the North Pole or the Equator. Design becomes part of the panorama.
CASSINA SHOWROOM 3800 NE Miami Court - Miami Design District, FL - Ph 305 576 3636 - www.cassinamiami.com
Quick Ship: delivery in 10 days. For product offering visit www.cassinausa.com or call 800-770-3568

December 3rd

Unveiling of Maarten Baas' exclusive pieces.
Berluti Store, Miami Design District,
Mosaic Building 161 NE 40th Street.

Jeremy Irons, initiated by Peter Sellers

Berluti

Paris

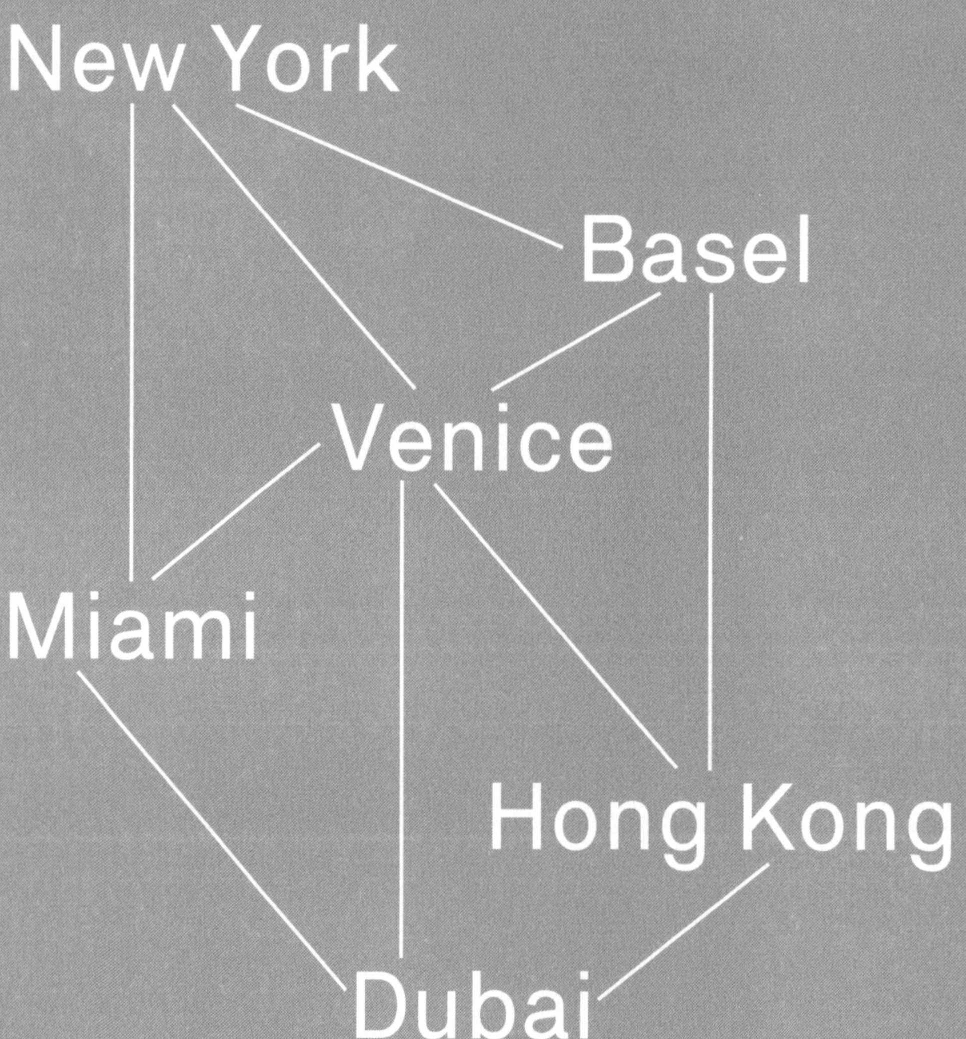

My Art Guides
Your compass in
the Art World
New York
Basel
Venice
Miami
Hong Kong
Dubai
On Paper, Web & App
Follow us on Facebook and Twitter
myartguides.com

W
HOTELS
DESIGNERS
OF
THE
FUTURE
AWARD

TOGETHER WITH
DESIGN MIAMI / BASEL,
W HOTELS HAS CREATED
A LAUNCHPAD FOR
RISING VISIONARIES
WHO SHARE OUR
PASSION FOR DESIGN.

WELCOME TO WHAT'S
NEW / NEXT.

#WDOF
WHOTELS.COM/DESIGN

IMAGE: BETHAN LAURA WOOD

©2013 Starwood Hotels & Resorts
Worldwide, Inc. All Rights Reserved.
W Hotels and its logos are the
trademarks of Starwood Hotels &
Resorts Worldwide, Inc., or its affiliates.

W
HOTELS
WORLDWIDE

ETTORE SOTTSASS

IMPORTANT WORKS FROM A PRIVATE COLLECTION

CHRISTIE'S
PRIVATE SALES

Exhibition in New York
December 7–20, 2013
Monday–Saturday, 10am–5pm
Sunday, 1–5pm

Venue
20 Rockefeller Plaza
New York, NY 10020

Contact
Simon Andrews
sandrews@christies.com
+ 44 (0) 77 4776 4341

ETTORE SOTTSASS (1917–2007)
Tondo, 1958 (detail)
for Il Sestante, enamel on copper
7.3/4 in. (20 cm.) diameter.

christiesprivatesales.com

MODERN
MAGAZINE
DESIGN
DECORATIVE ARTS
ARCHITECTURE
HOW TO GET MODERN
Subscribe online at www.modernmag.com
HOW TO BE MODERN
Contact modernadv@brantpub.com to advertise

Herzog & de Meuron *Hall 1 Süd* image courtesy Iwan Baan. Jonathan Muecke *Stabilizer* image courtesy Volume Gallery.
Apple, the Apple logo and iPhone are trademarks of Apple Inc., registered in the U.S. and other countries.
App Store is a service mark of Apple Inc.

TURON TRAVEL, INC.

2 Wooster Street, SoHo, New York, 10013
212-925-5453 / 800-952-7646
www.turontravel.com

Serving the Art World Since 1979

Art Fairs & Biennales
Quarterly eDirectory
Museum Groups & Art Specialist Tours

QVEST
A magazine about
fashion, culture & attitude
qvest.de

CASA
VOGUE
n.40
ECLECTIC

form
Design Magazine
Established 1957
form.de

Relaunch
Nº 250
as of October 2013

Self Advertisement

form is a magazine, devoted to the shaping of the visual, to the examination of the different forms of design, and to critical appraisal; this being based on a definite point of view.

form is concerned with the relations between the applied and the autonomous arts and with their relations to our life and to the objects of daily use.

form has as its viewpoint the conviction that we live in a technical age which seeks to express itself in the realm of visible forms but without having found its expression completely.

form views the world of visible form with this conviction in mind, eliminating what does not measure up and advocating that which does measure up.

form in other words is primarily concerned with the design of consumer goods, viewing design as related to the forms of the visual arts, of architecture but also of theater, film and photography.

form will primarily instruct; for this purpose gathering news from all over the world; the magazine is therefore indispensable for everyone who tries to keep up to date with recent developments.

form seeks to appear in a visual form that will present its material directly and forcefully supported by a not theorizing text.

Nos grandes lignes

form est un périodique se consacrant au façonnement des choses concrètes, étudiant les diverses formes possibles, jugeant avec un esprit critique et prenant chaque fois position.

form s'occupera par conséquent des rapports existant entre les arts appliqués et les arts libéraux et de leurs rapports avec notre vie et les objets d'usage courant.

form part du point de vue que nous vivons dans un âge technique cherchant ses formes d'expression dans le monde des formes concrètes, mais ne les ayant trouvées que partiellement.

form étudie, de ce point de vue, les phénomènes, choisit et prend fait et cause pour ce qui répond à ce point de vue.

form place par conséquent le façonnement des objets d'utilité au centre de ses préoccupations, considère leur façonnement industriel en rapport avec les formes de l'art plastique, de l'architecture, mais aussi avec celles du théâtre, du film et de la photographie.

form veut surtout informer, et entretiendra à cette fin des relations dans le monde entier. C'est pourquoi « form » sera un auxiliaire indispensable pour celui qui veut être orienté sur les créations vraiment nouvelles.

form cherche pour ces tâches une forme optique suggestive, qui présente le matériel sans ambages et le soutient sans mots inutiles.

form issue Nº 1, 1957

ARTS AND CULTURE IN MIAMI AND BEYOND.

THE MIAMI RAIL

Quarterly in print and online
www.MiamiRail.org

Top to bottom: **Lisa Elmaleh,** *Slash Pines*. Photo courtesy the artist and AIRIE Residency. **Hew Locke,** *For Those in Peril on the Sea*, 2011. Model boats and mixed media. Dimensions variable. Collection Pérez Art Museum Miami, museum purchase with funds from the Helena Rubinstein Foundation Challenge Grant. Reproduced with the permission of the artist. **Eve Sussman,** *Marilisa on the Floor*, 2005, Digital C-print, 39 1/2 x 51 inches. Private collection Richard J. Massey. Photo courtesy of The Bass Museum of Art. **Daniel Milewski,** *The Umpire*, 2012, Cork, wool, yarn, leather, wood, paint, 15.5 x 15.5 x 37.5 inches. Photo courtesy of Gallery Diet.

DESIGN BUREAU

NEW WORK FROM GANG, FOSTER, JAHN, & MORE P. 106

DESIGN BUREAU

TOYO ITO
THIS YEAR'S PRITZKER ARCHITECTURE PRIZE WINNER LOOKS AHEAD

HOT SHOTS
MEET THE PHOTOGRAPHERS WHO MAKE BUILDINGS LOOK BADASS

BUENOS AIRES
BIG-NAME DESIGNERS HEAT UP ARGENTINA'S MUST-VISIT CAPITAL

DUDES 'N DENIM
6 COOL JEAN JACKETS FOR FALL

THE ARCHITECTURE ISSUE

BUILDING THE FUTURE

10 BIG IDEAS
CHANGING THE WAY
WE LIVE, WORK, AND PLAY

OCTOBER 2013
$8 USA/CAN

+ THE LATEST ARCHITECTURE-INSPIRED FASHION, JEWELRY, FILMS, AND MORE

Get Cultured.

Available Quarterly and
Online at CulturedMag.com

READ THE LATEST IN
ARCHITECTURE, CULTURE & DESIGN.

DELIVERED TO YOU, WHEREVER YOU ARE.

Subscribe to *Metropolis* for the most ground–breaking design journalism in both print and digital editions.

metropolismag.com/subscribe

Design/Miami/ Design Log

Follow Design Log for exclusive coverage of Design Miami/ 2013's gallery shows, award commissions, Q A design talks and events.

Designmiamilog.com